R U D I
ENTERING
INFINITY

Rudra Press
P.O. Box 13390
Portland, Oregon 97213-0390
United States of America
Telephone: (503) 235-0175

Compiled and edited by Cheryl Berling Rosen
Cover design by Milton Glaser
Book design by Caroline Kutil
Typeset by Productivity Press

Manufactured in the United States of America

Library of Congress Cataloging-in-Publication Data

Rudrananda, Swami, 1928-1973
    Rudi: entering infinity/Swami Rudrananda (Rudi): foreword by
Swami Chetanananda: edited by Cheryl Berling Rosen.
        p.   cm.
    Includes bibliographical references and index.
    ISBN 0-915801-41-8
    I. Rosen, Cheryl Berling. II. Title III. Title: Entering infinity.
BL624.R7934   1994
294.5'44—dc20
                                            92-45648
                                                CIP

97 96 95 94   5 4 3 2 1

R U D I
ENTERING
INFINITY

Swami Rudrananda (Rudi)

Foreword by
Swami Chetanananda

Edited by
Cheryl Berling Rosen

Rudra Press

Portland, Oregon

Photo by Barry Kaplan

The more you grow spiritually, the further you go away from the earth. You begin to understand that there is no end and no limitation. Just as if you took off in a rocket ship, you finally see yourself diminish and disappear. And you are in space—deep inner space. This is infinity.

CONTENTS

INTRODUCTION

M any things made Rudi special. For instance, he was one of the first Americans to go to India and be initiated as a Swami in the Saraswati monastic order. This was a recognition of his work as a spiritual person. More important, however, was the capacity that underlay that recognition, namely the degree of his own contact with the creative energy of Life Itself. It was this capacity that allowed him to transmit the experience of that energy of Life to other people. And it was the purity within him which then allowed him to sustain his contact with those people, even as he took on their tensions and obstructions, and gave them an extraordinary teaching in return.

Rudi brought a practice to this country. It was an unusual practice, and not one that was intended to be easy. He first encountered it himself in the late nineteen-fifties, in his meeting with the Indian teacher, Bhagavan Nityananda. This took place in Ganeshpuri, near Bombay, where Nityananda had an ashram. The Bhagavan would come into a small room, lit by a few bare electric light bulbs, and would sit there quietly with his eyes open. People would come from near and far to see him because, in India, just seeing a spiritual teacher is considered a profound and important blessing, called darshan. So Nityananda would sit there with his eyes open, simply establishing a connection with each person who came according to their capacity to experience and sustain that contact.

This eyes-open practice is powerful and significant in the following sense: It trains us, with our eyes open, to see the world as it is. We see the diversity as it appears, not closing our eyes or retreating from it in any way. All of this diversity, for most people, is a source of confusion, of attraction, repulsion, ambivalence, pain and suffering, and of desire. But with our eyes open, we see into all of that and through it, to the fundamental power that underlies the entire field of our experience.

To do this means that we must become centered within ourselves—in other words, within this realm of diversity. We learn to open ourselves to its many pulsations and to the flow of creative energy that represents all of the interchange taking place in our lives and as our lives. This interchange is our life in a physical sense: We have to eat and drink. It is our life in an emotional sense: We have contact with others. It is our life in an intellectual sense: We collect, structure, and give forth information. And, finally, it is the Life of our lives.

In this eyes-open practice, we don't close ourselves off from, or deny, anything. Instead, we open ourselves fully to experience the source of all diversity, seeing through all that complexity to the fundamental, simple power that is the essence of all there is. Through this openness, we learn to take in every experience, not as reinforcements to the traumas in our lives but rather, as nourishment. In this way, we discover that there is no such thing as "a good thing" or "a bad thing." There is only nourishment, from which we grow. Good and bad experiences dissolve, and everything is nourishment in which our own vital force unfolds.

During the twenty-one years since Rudi's passing, the vital force that was the essence of his teaching has remained with us, undiminished. The particular flavor and form that he gave to it remind those of us who knew him of his presence every time we sit in meditation, every time we digest the tensions and pressures in our lives in the ways that he taught us to do. And within the teaching we received from him is the teaching that he, in turn, received from his teacher, Bhagavan Nityananda.

This book is composed of talks that Rudi gave to his students. They were recorded in 1972 and 1973 in the meditation room of his Manhattan brownstone on East 10th Street, and in his ashram in the Catskill Mountains at Big Indian, New York. When Rudi spoke, it was always following the teaching of open-eyed meditation class. His words were an extension of the flow of spiritual energy pulsating through him. From his own state of profound surrender, he would speak, planting seeds of understanding that would grow and flourish in the hearts of those around him.

It was Rudi's hard work and his sacrifice that make it possible for us to live in this inner dimension that he transmitted to us, to draw our whole lives from it and, in every way, to find ourselves and our experiences enriched. Even as we become simpler because of the joy we feel within ourselves, we find our lives becoming deeper and more alive.

This is possible because, with our eyes wide open to life, Rudi taught us to see through the diversity of the world to the infinite creative power that lies beneath it. We see the power that manifests as every human being in the world, as the tensions and traumas, the turmoils, hopes, and fears, and as all the uncertainty we face in our lives. We see it all. And in seeing it, feeling it, and having a living contact with that source of life, we find ourselves released from all the limitations of our lives into freedom.

Swami Chetanananda
1994

EDITOR'S NOTE

*T*he transmission of a teaching is a living thing. One could say that it costs the teacher his or her life. Therefore, the question of authorization is intrinsic to a teaching lineage of the kind into which Rudi poured his whole life. What is being transmitted is the entirety of that energy, that vital force. It is the teacher who determines who is prepared to sustain that force and pass it on, and who is not. He or she may train many students, but this is not equivalent to regarding them as ready to carry on that level of the work.

While Rudi was alive, he designated two people to teach under him: Swami Chetanananda, now in Portland, Oregon, and Stuart Perrin, now in New York. Before his passing, Rudi wrote a letter in which he assigned Swami Chetanananda the task of carrying on his work and taking over the direction of the ashrams he had established. Even now, any authorized teacher of Rudi's work must be someone directly connected with either Swamiji or with Stuart. Anyone else who claims to be a teacher trained by Rudi is self-proclaimed.

RUDI
ENTERING
INFINITY

CHAPTER 1

*O*nly by refining the atmosphere around us, by being able to absorb life consciously, does our state of being change. It is not consciousness, but rather an inner chemical process that finally comes about. Ultimately, what it is giving you is not a state of you or me, it is a state of being. It is the maturing of certain energies that have been flowing for many years.

Anything that is growing takes in a lower level of energy and converts it. This is the process of life. But we always give life and want to take life—and this is the wrong exchange. It's the wrong fuel. One should take death and give life. One should take negativity and give back a positive flow. In our stupidity, in our lack of ability to understand the creative processes, however, we reach for the wrong fuel. We reach for the wrong rewards. We reach without consciousness.

So we go along thinking that these things in the world recognized as rewards are the rewards for spirituality. But they're not. They are the rewards for the physical level. They are the things that the physical level claims are the rewards for its materialization. Yet on that level, this is the level of war, the level of vengeance, the level of all the things we claim we don't wish to be a part of.

When we are working for a spiritual life, why should we reach for the same reward and the same energy? We really have to understand the difference between the level of life and the level of spirituality.

* * *

When you feel free, when you feel that you can make a different commitment, when you have different values—then you have developed. This is why you should stop every few weeks, go deeply inside, and feel your relationship to what you want and to the distance that lies between you and what you want. You should periodically check your wish and your projections of what life has to offer. You will find that certain things have changed. You won't have to go to the movies once a week or have pizza or have somebody tell you that you have beautiful eyes. When you really are free of that, you can open and lift your sights.

* * *

When you find yourself caught up in external things, go deeper inside yourself. When there is a greater depth, there is a place to go—and it is not outside, it is inside. When you find that you are more superficial, it is because you have refused to go deeper inside. It is as if you were playing the piano and somebody was talking across the hall. If you were playing frivolously, you would be caught by it. But if you were playing something deep and demanding, would you hear it? I don't think so. Your superficiality allows you to be caught up in superficiality. You may not be interested in what you are playing, but you haven't worked deeply enough to bring yourself away from it. So stop playing "Chop-sticks" and start playing a concerto. Really go inside and make a dramatic effort to open.

Like attracts like. And a light effort attracts a light reward. Depth attracts depth. Longevity attracts longevity. A spiritual contract does not stipulate that you work one day and not the next. If this week you work and next week you don't, who will honor it? The contract is broken.

Understand that you have to earn your own respect. You have to feel value. But if you come here or anywhere else without opening deeply inside, you are not going to get. You should be here to drink very, very deeply. It is no different from a child taking milk from a mother's breast. You eat and eat and eat; you feel yourself getting full; you open and feel your flow. If you don't feel this flow surging through you, then you let it flow right out of you. It flows off the surface. This is the best way to recognize depth within yourself. If you feel this energy coming in, being absorbed and digested, and becoming part of your flow, then you are working very well.

* * *

Most people relate to their spiritual work without consciousness and to their ordinary lives with consciousness. Life—anything that you value in life, anything that you really do with consciousness—will bring you a reward. But people say, well, they can't do this and they can't do that. It's absolutely ridiculous. I know that when I used to travel in the Orient looking for art, from inside a taxi I could pick out a piece of sculpture on the fourth floor of a building. And people are like that; we are aware of external things. But if we can be sensitive to them, then we certainly should be sensitive to this higher thing. It is proof of how well we function on one level, and how badly we function on another, because we really don't care—or because we haven't made the effort to bring over values from one level to another.

We are all like this. We all have places where we register, where we really want, where we really have feelings. For instance, a prejudiced person can find somebody who has thirty percent Jewish blood four miles away or thirty percent Negro blood or five percent this or a Hungarian in the middle of the Sahara Desert—if they hate Hungarians. We have these instincts registering in us only for negative or primitive reasons. But we never think of taking that same equipment and raising it to a higher level.

We can raise the level of our equipment just by wanting to—but we don't want. We are waiting for somebody to come along and make it work out right. But if you are here, and you relate your energy to my energy, what has to happen to you? If you put your energy against my energy, it has to go up and up and up. It's like a tuning fork. This is what a rate of vibration is. You tune yourself against it. It's the same thing with the *om* sound, the audible vibration of creative energy. You listen to it, you tune yourself into it, and become one with the energy—because we really need a center. We can give out door prizes if you want, but there has to be something in you that consciously and creatively can take other areas of your life, put in a little inspiration, and raise their levels.

* * *

When you are given spiritual nourishment, it's like being given money. You can afford to see things. If I give you a hundred dollars, you can afford to go out and look at a pair of trousers, you can afford to look at a coat, you can afford to look at a lot of other things. But when you receive spiritual energy, you feel your tensions because of the richness that you are taking into yourself. You are being given nourishment that you can feel. When you work by yourself, you can't feel that.

It's a matter of product. When you're in a cheese store, you feel cheese. When you're in a bakery, you feel bread. You can only relate to what's around you. You can only take in what's being offered to you. And when I relate to art that I love, I get a great deal out of art. I get a great deal out of music, I get a great deal out of air, I get a great deal out of the sun, and I get a great deal out of water. And a million other things. I try to take from what I'm relating to—but I don't try to take out of water what I take out of art. It's a different thing.

And this is the stupid thing with people who over the years will talk about "so-and-so." I hear someone saying, "Well, I'm going to live with John, but Harry was wonderful." Harry was the last one, and then when she moves on to Freddy, she'll talk about John, and when she moves on to George, she'll talk about Freddy. People never learn to take from where they are and from what they are. They always want what was. They never grow and they spend their entire lives complaining.

When it's winter, love the winter; when it's summer, love the summer; when it rains, love the rain. I love every day and I am grateful every day. What I love in you, I love in you, and it's different than what I love in someone else. Why should I look for you in him and her in you? We refuse to find in a person that which is wonderful. We look for somebody or something else—as if we were looking for oysters in a cow cage. It doesn't exist and it's really very stupid.

It's the same if you see other spiritual teachers. It's completely ridiculous to relate them to me or me to them. Take the treasure that they offer and absorb and digest that. Then you can come back to take more from me. I'm not concerned because the whole reason is for you to grow. This is what life should be.

From wherever we are and whoever we're with, take what they have to offer. But along with the taking, be detached enough to feel the flow of energy wash the impurity out of the relationship. Don't become so attached to what you are relating to that you let go of the nourishment and become crystallized. Take the nourishment. Take it with great openness and great consciousness. Feel with and talk to that person, and be detached enough to feel the flow and do your breathing exercise. Otherwise, you will find yourself completely limited because the body can only assimilate a certain amount of creative energy. The rest should wash out, just like excess vitamins.

* * *

Consciousness has to do with making a conscious effort. The body automatically absorbs, digests on a physical level, and throws off ninety-nine percent of everything that isn't right. Because you also absorb spiritually and psychically, you have to consciously break down and wash out the flow. To grow with another human being means to grow in a conscious way and feel the flow of creative energy. If you don't—you will get the crystallization, not the nourishment. You will get the limitation, not the energy

You should only take in the energy and grow—and the other person should grow. If we limit ourselves because of our lack of consciousness, we don't feel this flow within. And this flow allows me to sit with all of my students over and over and not get crippled. I would die of cancer in six weeks if I did not have that. You get cancer in a lot of places in your system. You crystallize when you become ineffective in your ability to take because you don't allow this creative flow to work through you. And that is happening all the time. This energy is coming down and trying to flow through you to release all the tensions and poisons inside.

This is like a chain that you have to pull consciously. Every single day you sit down, hang your hands down at your side, take a deep breath into your heart, and say, "I wish to surrender negative psychic tensions." Consciously let this flow come through you. Take another breath and pump out of you all of the tensions that have accumulated within you psychically. If you make the conscious effort, you will feel it pour out of you like scum. And if you haven't done it, you had better start doing it every single day. If you can, do it after your breathing exercise. Take a very deep breath and you will feel this stuff coming out of you.

In growing, the thing that holds us from level to level is this kind of psychic glue. We grow and we stretch and then we stop working and we go down again because this adhesive, this inner gook, is not destroyed. If you don't break it down consciously, you will never be free. You will finish your work, and six weeks later you will be right back where you were. You have to break down this adhesive that is part of the brain connection and consciously let this stuff flow out. And you will feel it.

* * *

Growing and changing requires breaking down the structure—and it has to be done consciously. Finally, you surrender. You really surrender. You say, "I'm going to let go," and then try to open and let this thing flow. You say, "I want to let go" and it's just like being crippled, nothing in you wants to, because you really don't want to let go. This is what you all must find when you sit down and say, "I really wish to let go inside, I really wish to surrender." Open and let this stuff out and you will find how your heart doesn't want to pump it out. Inside, you don't want to change, you really want to stay the same. You want the security of complaining and complaining and not changing. Within yourself, you must realize that you have to consciously want to change. You must consciously ask for it.

This flow comes from God, this creative flow in you will break down and allow the change. You can take everything apart. But to keep it apart and to destroy it, you have to take the adhesive or bonding away. The bonding, the molecular structure within us has to be washed out consciously. If you don't consciously break down the bonding day after day, you will go back into the same pattern. The bonding or molecular structure is only broken down through your consciousness and through your will. You say, "I know I can't live with it and I find it hard to let go, but here it goes anyway." Then you open. And all the little things start to go out of you and you cannot put it back together again the way it was. That is magic. It's the stuff that holds all of these other things together. And until you deeply let go, the pattern will never wash out.

We are chained unconsciously to our patterns because we have never pulled or flushed out of us the stuff that holds them together. This understanding is vital. If you work and earn the change, but it never takes place, or if you move from a shabby one-room apartment to a twenty-room house, but you prefer your one-room apartment, ask yourself why. This thing in your brain has never allowed itself to expand and move. You live like a beggar your whole life because you can't surrender the insecurity. You can't surrender the patterns of your former life. So your chemistry can't change, this sweetness can't come in, this state of being cannot expand itself within you. Our materialism—this thing in us that grabs and holds on—keeps us prisoners. Therefore, we don't enjoy the things that we've attained. Nothing in us can expand and there's no sweetness we can take.

* * *

When something turns from starch to sugar, it takes place inside. This remarkable process is called ripening. Within us, this ripening can take place only when we surrender the starchy, immature part of our lives and allow our consciousness to grow and this ripening and sweetness to take place. This freedom, this joy, can take place. We don't just act like happy people—we are happy. It is a state of being, not a state of acting. This thing flows out of us and we become happy. We feel it. It radiates out of us. Nothing is worse than somebody with a lot of money trying to act successful, trying to act happy, trying to act secure. Because it has never taken place inside them, they can never share an enlightenment.

Try to break down your tensions every day after your breathing exercise. The first time you do it, do it for half an hour. Ask deeply to surrender negative psychic tensions. Feel this thing that binds you, this stuff that holds you between levels, and let it come out of your body. You are breaking down the little things that attack all of your energies. If you break down, you can expand in your exercise. Otherwise, you're working from 1 to 2, and then down to 1 and then back to 2, and you do this for the next hundred years. You'll never get to 3 unless you break down the molecular structure that holds these things together.

That's what stops so many people. They're going out and gathering, they're going out and gathering information, they're gathering wisdom. And what happens? They become crystallized because the substance within them accumulates just like grease on a stove and makes the instrument ineffective. It can no longer work because this stuff builds up and the mechanism gets stuck. It has to be scraped off and washed away. And the only way this can take place is with consciousness.

We live with so much of our mechanism encrusted that it's ineffective. So whatever you want or whatever you attain, that's fine. I wish you every success in the world. But when you get it, be sure that you can enjoy it.

You can only enjoy it by breaking down from where you were to where you are. Only when your mechanism is clean can you expand and really enjoy.

CHAPTER 2

I am not interested in having an outer form or an outer characteristic or an outer manner. The energy is really a feeding and should be free of form. As it comes through different channels, it will emerge differently.

A diamond reflects light by the way it is cut. And God has cut every one of us individually. So trying to stylize, to crystallize people to reflect a certain pattern of energy or a certain way of giving, becomes an extraordinary limitation. I give you the way I can give. This doesn't mean that another teacher would give you more or less. It means that they would give you differently. And the reason to study with a teacher is for you to grow—not to force a teacher to find a way of stylizing and limiting you.

Each person gives you something else—one represents vitamin C, another vitamin B, and me vitamin X. Nourishment is the issue. Somebody else will explain the breathing exercise and you will find a new insight because of the way that person's diamond has been cut or the way that person is an instrument for the force. This really isn't a contradiction—it is an expansion of the same force. The force simply comes out in a different way, it comes out in a different pattern, it comes out in a different energy. From different people, it emerges lighter or heavier or deeper or more superficial. But there are times for light rain and there are times for heavy rain and there are times for snow and there are times for all of these different aspects of the same thing.

Within ourselves, we have to be easy and secure and realize that we take, in a teaching or in receiving, only what we can absorb. Thinking about it is just a game. Take it in. Let it be absorbed. What you don't want will pass out of your body. So when you get involved in your mind with a lot of thinking and decide that what the teacher says is a contradiction—remember. Remember it is just you looking to play that kind of game.

* * *

You should come out of meditation or one of my lectures and remember nothing, absolutely nothing. It should all have passed through you. What needs to be absorbed will be absorbed and a week later you may find yourself in a situation and suddenly a voice will say something. Or this line of thinking will come up and you will suddenly understand. It is similar, in a sense, to becoming computerized. This spiritual wealth keeps coming in and your system becomes free to flow. Within the flow's mass of energy and material you will find your answers. You will not find them by restricting what goes in—that is being stuck in your mind.

The whole reason for working is to expand and allow this flow to take place. To turn your mechanism into a kind of great cosmic computer taking in energy from the atmosphere, from people, from everything. Without restriction. It will be assimilated as it is needed, which has nothing to do with your will. It has to do with God's will, or the creative will that only encompasses what is natural to itself. The body rejects anything foreign put inside.

There is really nothing to analyze. It is just to take in and take in, and what you can't hold will pass out of you. You will never have to be responsible for it because it will take care of itself. You are working for a state of your own being—not for a state of Rudi or of anybody else. You free yourself by the simple act of taking in energy and surrendering. You automatically absorb what is needed. And what is not needed will fall away.

* * *

I'm not interested in your ideas or what you think or don't think. I'm not even very interested in my own ideas. So why should I be caught up in your thinking? If you have a problem or think you see something another way, fine—you can express it. We all can learn in this way. It adds to the total information. But your expression should not come out wearing a little smile of knowing or superiority. The only thing that counts is to open and expand and surrender and increase the flow within you.

The thing that crystallizes a person is a lack of flow. The flow of energy comes in and washes through you. It washes out the imperfections and impurities and prevents you from crystallizing. The thing that limits a person's growth is the mind. The mind sorts out and begins to attack the material that comes through. And because it can't absorb so much built-up tension, the mind eventually crystallizes. By increasing the volume and depth of the flow, you are purified. It is like a sewer that washes through and takes out all the imperfections. We don't know right from wrong anyway, so let it take care of itself. This extraordinary thing is made to take care of itself. The saying "The mind is the slayer of the soul" is true if we let it function as a thinking and operable thing. If surrendered, however, the mind can take in any amount of material and never get stuck because its parts don't break down. They expand and expand and expand.

What eventually kills people is that we go here and somebody says one thing, then we go there and another person says something different. This makes lines going across and up and down that begin to make a fabric, a fabric more like steel mesh than cloth. Everything gets caught in it and, before we know it, there is no flow. It doesn't matter what somebody says. It only matters whether we can digest it. If we can digest it, we can absorb and take its content. Spiritually, we are working for that.

We are not trying to become authorities on each other. We are here to grow and die and transcend ourselves over and over and over again. But the need in our own minds to always be right and to understand things is the ego. If we really know anything we should know that things will change and change and change. If we can surrender inside ourselves the need to know, the need to have this kind of security that thinks it knows, then we have the one essential principle for spiritual work and ordinary life: the cycle of death and rebirth and death and rebirth.

* * *

Our psychic system is like a plant sitting in the ground. When it feels rain, it reaches out and absorbs the water. New roots grow out and spread. It's a very casual, natural thing. You don't find a plant screaming, jumping up and down in any way, and disturbing its potential. It manifests its potential by assimilating whatever energy and whatever nourishment come to it. And it grows.

You must understand that your sitting here with me has to do with assimilating, taking in nourishment, and growing. If you are not breathing consciously, having your attention inside, feeling these muscles moving and absorbing and digesting, then nothing is happening. It is like sitting in water. This thing will stay on the bottom. Since it is not rising and circulating, the energy and information you are given will lay there and rot. It will lay at your feet until eventually you get gangrene. You have to take and absorb and really feel this thing expanding in you. Feel the energy come down from the mind, pass through all the chakras to the base of the spine, and move up your spinal column. It is essential. Otherwise, you sit and listen and agree or disagree and go through a whole number. But this is not what it is all about. It is to feel the flow of your energy inside and absorb it.

As you grow, you will transcend yourself and everything you are concerned about. Your problems will be drawn into you by this root system just like a tree. It will go up and up and all the problems you think you have, or that you are born into, will disappear to be absorbed as energy. And so, being concerned about anything has to do with your mind. You haven't learned to live quietly and be grateful for those problems.

Your problems represent natural resources. This is what you are given to break down and turn into fertilizer. Really good human beings never study spiritual work because they don't have enough raw material to break down. Studying and growing have to do with breaking down and changing over energy from one level to another. And nice people don't have spiritual lives because they were born without this chemistry, without this ability to break down and transmit one energy into another. So, when you find yourself talking to someone about your "spiritual thing," it's ridiculous. It has nothing to do with reality because it's not their reality, it's not their potential. How can you open a cotton mill unless you have cotton to put through these different carding processes? You need raw material.

* * *

Spiritual work is like running a factory. You need tons of raw material to burn, break down, and package. And when you finish it, you start over again. You bring what you just packaged to the front of the line, put it back into the machine, and tear it apart. You are refining the same energy endlessly. This is the whole principle. You never run out of resources because you can always take what you refine and use it again as raw material. Your product goes back to become raw material because the very nature of life is that things change.

The principle of existence is that nothing is on the market for more than six months as a usable product. The body can counteract any kind of positive change in a very short time. If people who grow and achieve stop growing, they become antiques. They die because the force within them is not transmittable in a living way. Either you are growing, refining your energy, and having a vital flow inside, or you are walking around as something that should be put in a museum case. You cannot give life unless you take in more material to break down and refine. For even the most brilliant physicist, principles of physics change. Principles of biology change. New laws of nature that destroy the whole system are continually being discovered. In that sense, spirituality is not different than anything else. What is discovered today will make everything that existed until today ridiculous.

So, thinking that you are going to retire in a year or five years and be realized is garbage. It doesn't work that way. Either you are growing, being broken down, and being recycled all the time, or you will never have a spiritual life. Instead, you become some kind of spiritual egomaniac inflicting your limitations on others. The wonderful thing about spirituality is that it uses the same energy over and over to make a new vitality. Your life can be vital. It can be exciting. It can be brilliant. Who wants to sit on the same egg endlessly and feel secure? Only a sick and limited being.

You have the potential to open and feel the difference in the atmosphere. It is like walking into a garden and smelling a rose and a daisy and a geranium. They each have different smells, they each have different textures, and the energy that comes in is different all the time. You should have this feeling when you wake up in the morning. Lie there and feel the day. Open yourself and try to feel the energy. Feel what is coming into the atmosphere, tune into it. Lie there for a minute and say, "I have a new day. Where am I? How am I?"

You can go to sleep happy and wake up like a moron or a tiger with a harpoon in its side. You are not the same person that went to sleep, because over the past six or eight hours everything that came into the atmosphere changed. Consistently trying to have a "lovely day," walking around snapping their fingers and singing reduces people to the level of cows. They have put themselves into a state of "consistent spirituality" and there is no such thing. You are dealing with people who have hypnotized themselves. The energy coming into the atmosphere is continually changing. If you want to reach a level that is constant, become a cow or a dog. But human beings are not here to feel like cows or plants or anything else. We should reflect the changing energy that comes in and the changing drama about to be played in our lives. We will see things differently.

We do not have to be crystallized as people. We are not limited nor do we need to be limited to see things that way. If someone is a bastard, tell yourself he is a bastard. Why paint him and everyone else white or pink because you want to think that you are living in a world that is white or pink. It's ridiculous. An ordinary animal can smell its enemy. A human being should likewise feel what is dangerous, what is real, what can be encompassed, what should be opened to, and what you are opening to. Everything is not the same. This need to reduce your mind to a cow's mind where everything is wonderful and everyone is beautiful is not real. Be free.

* * *

*D*on't look for perfection in me. If someone ever says something about me, it might be true—but it has nothing to do with what I teach and how I teach. I'm not concerned with being perfect. I want to acknowledge my own imperfection and not inflict it on anyone unnecessarily. I want to understand that it is part of the endlessness of my own growth. When I need to be perfect, I'll be perfect. But it's absolutely useless at this stage in your life with all of the shit piled up in your closet to walk around and try to kid yourself about your perfection.

Out of the raw material you break down, you grow and absorb the energy. You work yourself from inside out, tearing out, destroying, and finding a sense of nothingness. That nothingness allows God to come in. But this somethingness—ego and prejudices and limitations—is your raw material. If you process and refine it all, you can open consciously. Otherwise, you will never come to anything that represents yourself. A man who thinks he has a spiritual life is really an idiot. Until you can surrender yourself to open and see everything that's inside you, you can never approach God. You are working to see your nothingness a million different ways. But how can you surrender yourself when you don't even know who you are? The only thing that can create a oneness inside you is the ability to see more of yourself as you work every day to open deeper and say, "Fine, I'm short-tempered" or "I'm aggressive" or "I love to make money" or "I have no feeling for anyone else." Once you recognize that you are all of these things, they will be connected in you. You will finally be able to take a breath and allow these things to open. You can surrender them and you can surrender yourself.

Until you are conscious of that oneness as well as your limitations, you can't have a real spiritual exercise. You can't open what is not yours to open. So your self-image, the ego that protects you, is the thing that prevents you from having a spiritual practice. You can't give away something you don't have. And unless you have control, this thing can never be surrendered.

People will go and study something like "mind control." They build on top of what they have without first having control of what is underneath. Building something on top of what you are does not make you a free person—it makes you a pile of garbage with one inch of snow on top. You can control the snow, you can even melt the snow, but underneath it is this mountain of yourself. You have to be able to dig through the middle of the mountain, split it down the middle, and open it up. Only then do you have what you can call an open mind. You can feel this mountain cut right from the top to the bottom and open. You have to do this with yourself.

* * *

*E*very time you do the breathing exercise, you are going deeper and deeper inside until you can open yourself. It is like cutting an apple in half. You can feel your heart and every muscle in your body open, not from the surface tensions that you work from, but from a depth where you go deeper inside and say, "I wish to surrender." It's like stroking a pussycat. You stroke the surface and align certain things, but you haven't gotten inside. To get inside, to surrender, you must ask deeply, and then deeper and deeper and say, "Hey look, I'm not here to protect myself. I really wish to surrender." Go inside like somebody diving into a pool from a hundred feet. Cut right through and touch the bottom.

As you work every day, keep asking to make a deeper commitment and feel yourself opening deeper. Either you are working deeper and deeper in yourself, or you are on the surface playing games. This is what spirituality is about.

* * *

When you wake up in the morning, the first thing to do is tune into the day. Lie there in bed, keep your eyes closed, and feel inside. First, see if you can feel inside. If not, take a breath and feel what this inner beast is doing, whether there is something in you that can open up to a spiritual life—or is it screaming.

Don't carry yesterday's garbage into today. Don't start your day off with reasons and complaints and fights. If you do, you are going off armed for the day—not in a state of surrender. You are allowing all the things coming to the surface to go underground; you will wake up and get to them during the day. They will come out as aggression against other people. But if you lie there and begin to feel all the little complaints, you can say, "Look, this is ridiculous, I've only just begun the day! If I start like this, what will the rest be?"

Instead, begin to break them. Open and surrender those things consciously so that if they do come up, you can say, "Here I am bringing up six o'clock in the morning." These things are just looking for a fight. Or you lie there and suddenly feel, "My God, it's a beautiful day and I feel great." You have good feelings inside. You can expand while you are brushing your teeth. While you shower, you can expand and feel something good. You can destroy whatever negative tensions are there by consciously breaking them down or, if you have a positive feeling, by opening. You are expanding whatever energy is there and using it in the most wonderful way possible. You know the direction your day will go in.

There are days when I wake up and hear "clink, clink"—and I know it will be a very good day for business. Or I know that tremendous things have happened in my sleep, and I can absorb and digest and expand them. The reason to tune in in the morning is to expand whatever energy is going in a right direction and to surrender, break, or destroy the things that are trying to catch you. Start the day with consciousness and with some sense of what you are and what you want. Then, when somebody says something that rubs you the wrong way, it doesn't become a reason to express the anger you had earlier. If they say something terrible and you wake up feeling wonderful, you can be above it. You can give them a kiss and a hug and turn them around. Use the beginning of your day to consciously manipulate your energy.

If you can take your energy and begin to move it, you begin to have a sense of form, a sense of direction, and a sense of reason. It works for you. You don't wake up with this madness in you and inflict it on everyone else. Yes, the madness may be there. So, when your breakfast eggs come upside down instead of sunnyside up, you look at them and think, "Boy, they are really trying to make me fight." So you reverse the direction.

Learn to use energy in a simple way—with consciousness. You can use energy as a tool. And when the phone rings and somebody says your car was stolen, well, you think, "This is the day somebody steals my car. Is it going to happen on a day that I'm feeling wonderful? Of course not." And you mentally begin to shape and form and move these forces. I mean, the day somebody calls me to complain is the same day six people call me to complain. These things build. And if you can look at it and be above it, you can say, "Isn't that wonderful." It has nothing to do with you, because you have consciously made your day higher than that. Or if it's a fantastic day, you have consciously made it that.

You begin to see the direction and the pattern of energy. You know that if things are going badly, that's the day your mother will call to say her boyfriend fell and broke a foot or somebody is not going to return your tools. Be prepared. You can see the direction the day is taking and know that these things are there to test you. It's not a day for you to be tested and lose—it is a day for you to be above it. Of course, by the end of the day you will probably pass out from exhaustion. You go to sleep exhausted, but not crushed. This is the principle of transcending energy. You learn how to work above the energy, not confront it and get caught.

* * *

Who says spiritual work, or any kind of conscious work, has to be anything but a lot of fun? It doesn't have to be a serious, dogged kind of thing. You should enjoy it. You should have a sense of drama. You should have a sense of vitality. And more than anything else, you should have a sense of its endlessness. It doesn't have to be one way. It doesn't have to be sitting there in a position you saw in a movie. It isn't necessary. It's like riding a wave in Hawaii. If the wave comes at an angle, do you always go the same way? You carry the flow of the energy and you surf that way. You know how to jump it, you know how to ride it, and you know how to keep on top of it. Well, this is what spirituality is about. You learn the direction of the energy coming into you. You work with it, you study it, and then you go out and have a great day. Regardless of what is coming in, your day will be great, it will be dramatic. You become one with this flow of energy, you go boom, boom, boom, and you make yourself a very good day. It is not sitting there saying, "Oh, my astrology chart says today isn't supposed to be very good, so I have to lock myself in the closet." It's ridiculous.

It's the way you ride your day—and you must ride it creatively by knowing what you have to work with. You dress accordingly and you act accordingly. But if you try to fight a force that is coming in this direction because you want to go to the right and the force is coming in from the right, you are going to get smashed. You will get pulled into the undertow. Work along with the direction of that day's energy. Lie there in the morning and feel it come in, feel the direction, feel your attitude. You know what you have to do.

So, when your eggs come upside down and you wanted them sunnyside up, you say, "Here I am, crazy today. If I'm willing to put that kind of energy into a pair of eggs, then I really am a nut." Then you can sit down and eat the eggs and shut your mouth. You can incorporate that extraordinary energy that would have gone out on those eggs. You can sit there and watch yourself go through this little drama and, because you are a little above it, you can turn the eggs over, eat them, and expand. The energy that would have gone out that way is coming into you. You have incorporated it into your being, and you walk out like you did the greatest thing in the world. You didn't hit someone over the head for turning your eggs the wrong way.

This is the real way to work spiritually. It is not small—it is very, very big.

* * *

We make tensions because we don't know how to live and grow. We make tensions. We have energy that we have to spend. We are, in a sense, born every day with this wealth that we think we have to spend. But we never think of saving. It goes out, it goes out, it goes out. But if we work consciously, we transcend ourselves and this wealth comes through us and rises to the top of our heads. It nourishes us and we grow.

* * *

If you stand and fight with your mother every day, you're not going to learn anything. Only when you can detach from it and slowly rise, can you begin to learn. I mean, it took me twenty-five years to figure that out. I was getting less and less crazy, and less and less tense, and I finally saw, "This is the way my mother operates." She makes those tensions because she can't express herself in any other way. I don't intend to be involved with them.

A lot of people live making tensions. It is the only way they know and it is the only product they have for their energy. Some husbands and wives spend forty or fifty years fighting. This is the way they express their emotions. They fight and they fight and they fight. And you can't even tell them that they are fighting because they don't even know they are fighting. A lot of the world is like that. I mean, go to the United Nations and listen to the silliness that goes on there. If they sat down, in fifteen minutes they could say, "Look, we'll give you a piece of this, and you can have a piece of that." They are only sitting there buying and selling all day long. It's like a stock market, except countries and power are involved. It's the same thing, just another marketplace. But they can't express it openly because it is not how people deal with each other in this world. To transcend it means that they wouldn't be able to walk around wearing uniforms and have parades. They are just like children. A little army marching here and another one over there. And the fact that millions of people are getting killed is completely incidental. They identify more with the games.

The thing is, you can have a wonderful life and live beautifully and dramatically. You don't have to be a beast or an alcoholic or a nut. There is no reason for excessive anything. You can live and grow and enjoy—and have a spiritual life.

Living and spirituality are not a contradiction. Although it's become a thing where, to have a spiritual life, you are expected to cut off your hands and feet and nose and every other appendage. It's ridiculous. Energy that is not used is lost. Use it consciously. And the best way is to start your day consciously. Feel what your energy is. Feel the direction you are going in and then use your breathing exercise to consciously stay above it. Don't react if someone turns to a jazz station on the radio and they know you love classical music. Don't let it become a thing where you think someone is deliberately trying to drive you crazy. No one is trying to drive you crazy. Maybe she turned on the radio and went into the bathroom and it's playing jazz by accident. Do you have to demand a formal three-page letter of apology? People do these things. They go crazy over nothing. But if you can see your energy for the day and the direction it's going in, you can really work it more consciously.

* * *

*I*f you are a big enough person to make a concession, you can turn everything around. Later you can say, "I thought about what you said two days ago, and you know, it was really brilliant. You were right." And the conversation and the energy just go "wump!" and reverse direction. If you are big enough to say "I'm sorry" or be open and give someone a compliment, you can take a situation and turn it around.

You get carried along because you haven't made an effort or the other person's energy is stronger than yours. But don't forget, it is very easy to put out your foot and trip someone. It doesn't take much effort. It isn't a question of being dramatic, it's a question of being simple.

To turn it around, I have to pull myself back, I have to surrender, I have to transcend, I have to do everything. Do you think someone else is going to do it for me? To have a better life or to be a superior human being means making superior sacrifices. It doesn't mean making demands from other people. If I am stronger than you, should you apologize to me? No, I should apologize to you. I am happy to apologize to you if it saves you energy. I am not going to wait for you to apologize to me because life just isn't long enough. So what? So you say to somebody something that will turn the situation around. Then you can feel a real flow between yourself and the other person. You can say to someone who's being an absolute horse's ass about a lot of things, "I really understand and it's very wonderful. Would you like to have a cup of coffee?" You just break it, get the cup of coffee, and sit down. And you say, "Look at this vase I just bought" or something.

People are glad to be let off—and you don't have to kick them in the guts to do it. They also want it to end, but they don't know how to end it. A lot of things in life are like this. For many people and situations you're involved with, it can't end until it falls apart because the momentum has begun. You have to stop it some way. You can say, "Look, I can't stand this anymore." But to say, "He started it, let him take care of it" is stupid. He can't take care of it, he's caught by it. You pick up the person and put him on your lap and say, "I love you" and it stops it. You are also saying to yourself, "I also love my energy, and I love this chance to grow by stopping a bad situation."

These situations occur because of the desire to win. That is the principle behind war. "We can kill them." Meanwhile, we lose three million people but they lose four million, so we win. What kind of winning is it? Everything is that way in life. It's a basic thing of "We're going to win" or "I am better than you." It's to the death. "And if I don't win, I die honorably."

What kind of honorable death is that? It's proof that you are stupid, because you'll have to come back and do it all over again. So back you come to do it again and again and again. What kind of principles are those? You're spending fifty thousand years in the same rat race going around and around. You come here like a rat, you ring a bell, the food comes out, and you think you are well-trained. You have to break the pattern and not sustain it in any way. This has to do with becoming free. You have to become free of this flow of karma, this thing of going out and touching everything. You stop and turn it around. By stopping the karma from extending horizontally, you throw it up and turn it into a ladder. With the same energy, you can climb to a higher level instead of going around in circles.

CHAPTER 3

*T*he ecology of human beings is that we live in our own garbage and poison the atmosphere with it. You have to open beyond yourself. You have to do more than take a breath and open a little. You have to gradually open more and more so that you get outside your own immediate atmosphere. You all sit in about a foot and a half of electricity or energy that is the contact between your soul and this creative flow. Each time, you have to ask inside to open deeper and deeper, to feel this opening, and go deeper until you feel as if you are drilling a hole inside. When you open, you are really breaking down outer tension. It is like a coconut. Inside you have the milk and outside you have the capacity to break through the shell. If you just keep touching the surface and making feeble efforts, you will never break down all the stuff that keeps you from living.

* * *

*A*ll of our organs and muscles are limited by the tremendous tension within us that comes not only from this life, but from past lives. From our parents, from our culture, from our religion and race, we take a little of the energy and all of the tensions. This means that we live on very little nourishment. We find all kinds of cultures represented in our lives and in our pasts, but always the *tension* of this culture. We never dig inside for the energy. Instead, we either accept or reject everything that we are without experiencing it. The prejudices within us represent the total accumulation of our pasts that we have been unable to open to. So, when we reject somebody or when we find someone that we can't feel a flow with, we are really rejecting ourselves. When we hate somebody, we are hating ourselves. This is why we talk about the compassion of the Buddha, meaning that he felt love for everybody. He never denied anybody, he never rejected anybody. We must realize that with things we can't relate and open to, we must be quiet. We absolutely have to save our energy and grow stronger inside. And as we grow inside, as we open more and take in more nourishment, we will break down those walls around us one at a time.

* * *

A lot of what we experience in life represents our inability to release tension. We can't get anywhere because we stand by it, look at it, find it convenient. We really don't want to break it down right now. And we make excuses. We talk about how beautiful that wall is and how necessary it is because it holds something back and serves a purpose. It's crazy. You have to go in there, take an ax, and give it a whack. Once you start, it breaks down. But we all become psychic architects. We build these walls and go around saying how fabulous they are and look at the style, the design, the texture. We're talking about things that shouldn't exist. But because they do exist, we make a science of fooling ourselves about how wonderful this resistance is. We start talking about it as if it was something extraordinary—when it is stupidity. We start discussing things that represent garbage instead of looking and saying, "All right, it's garbage. It exists." It's true that we may not be able to do anything about it, but we don't have to give it credibility. We don't have to stucco it, put barbed wire on top, and install doors and windows.

* * *

If you find in yourself something that you can't do, say, "Fine, this is a pile of garbage that I don't have the energy to face today." Then go to sleep early. Try to meditate a little more. Say, "I'm going to get up in the morning and rip the hell out of it." But don't start building fantasies around it. Don't embroider it. Don't do all kinds of other jobs with it. If you are a coward, you are a coward. If you're a freak, you're a freak. Look at it, accept it, and say, "This is part of my insanity and I understand it." Don't justify it by saying, "When I'm forty years old, I'm going to get rid of it" or "When I'm sixty years old, I'm going to get rid of it" or "When I'm . . ."

You are living with it today. Can you use it constructively in the flow of your growth? Does it add to it or does it take away tremendously? If it takes away, then start to break it down. Talk quieter. Act quieter. Be a little more reserved. Open more, really enjoy, and take energy out of it. This is the important thing. It doesn't matter what the wall is or, if you begin to mine it, what the mountain is. If you draw energy from it, you start to get life out of it. And if you're getting life out of it, you will eventually destroy it. But when you look at it as a great pillar of magnificence and start worshipping it, then you are really in trouble. If you have a capacity to make tensions in one place, then draw out of it something real. If you are a voyeur, go outside and watch birds. Turn it into something less tense that gives you more pleasure and gets you out into nature. It's a real way of growing.

* * *

Most people make monuments out of their blocks. Once, at my store, I had a customer who was a good-looking young man. He was healthy and vigorous and taught karate. And unusual—he was Puerto Rican with wavy, blond hair, a nice guy with a nice way of walking. After he was in about six or seven times, he said, shyly, because he had no one else to ask, "What about sex and celibacy?"

I said, "You know, I was waiting for you to ask." Because I could feel it in him. He said for three years he hadn't touched a girl. I said, "How often did you before?"

"Well, once in six months."

"Sure," I said. "You're now taking an inadequacy and making a monument out of it."

He was inadequate, he wasn't qualified, he wasn't anything else, so suddenly this became a tribute. And he started to laugh.

I said, "It shows on you." You could see on him the fact that he never had this kind of passion. He never had this kind of depth or even the interest. So, it wasn't a tribute, he was hiding behind his inadequacy.

Endless numbers of married couples have come to study with me. Maybe one partner or both of them were bored with the other. So, the one who was more inclined to non-functioning suddenly would use his or her spiritual life as a reason to not function with the partner. It's disgusting. It's a way of hiding behind something else. You don't kill something to grow. You expand, live more, and become more disciplined with it. But don't stop functioning. To function creatively, to expand your energy, and to grow is fantastic. And while there are times when celibacy is a healthy thing, it has to be done consciously and not as a way of retreating from life.

And this kid was remarkable that way. It was written on him very clearly that this was his way of retreating from life, not his path to finding it. He was sublimating this and making himself into something very different. It was a weakness in him. And then, of course, he brought a couple of other people to meet me. And he brought in his exact opposite, another fellow teaching karate in the Bronx who was also Puerto Rican. This guy looked like a black Orpheus and Charles Atlas combined. He could knock down people all over the place. No one could touch him as a teacher—and he was sexy. So I said, "Well, if he can do this and you both had the same teacher, where is this right and that wrong?"

It isn't, it is a matter of individual choice. And these are the kinds of lies that prevail in people. We allow something to crystallize us because it is convenient. Nothing should crystallize us. If we don't want to do something, don't. But whether or not we do this or do that has nothing to do with anything. It should not stop our creative flow and our spiritual flow. It shouldn't make a difference whether we are functional or non-functional. It is a question of energy.

* * *

*I*n the Hindu tradition, everything is *maya* or tremendous illusion. And it is very true. There are enormous amounts of illusion on every level and in every aspect of a person. So we must be careful not to study something that feeds our illusions in any way. A spiritual practice should always break them down and make realities. These things should come into our being. And more than anything else we have to be able to open more, take in more energy, and feel a greater flow of force. This will free us. It will free us of everything. And it is the nourishment that we live with that gives us the capacity to do our spiritual work.

CHAPTER 4

When you enter into a relationship with a teacher or a master or anyone at all, you will find one thing in common—all are different. They all have a different vibration and a different energy. You have to enter every relationship with openness, because unconsciously and automatically you start setting up a pattern. You think it is running to the right or to the left or it is looking up, and it's not. You have to become sensitive to the way the flow is coming in, to the way the energy is manifesting. If you pick huckleberries one day and apples the next day, you will be on completely different levels. These forces are on different levels and they have different depths. They have different ways of manifesting and different ways of entering your being.

The purpose of spiritual growth is to break patterns. In your breathing exercise, you have to stop making patterns. When you start turning your exercise into a ritual, you are really creating an idol in yourself and demeaning God. It is the endless and everlasting way this thing comes that is the challenge. You must be open to receive it the way that it wants to come—not the way that you wish to receive it. People lose ninety-nine percent of what

comes because they want it to come from the right on
Monday and from the left on Tuesday and this way and
that way. They are filled with all kinds of ritual without
the sensitivity to be open. It can break your heart because
it is a changing flow with a different density. It comes in
many ways and in different forms and in different fields
of energy. If you are sensitive to whatever you feel, if you
feel the change in it, you can begin to work in more and
more ways.

It is not one pattern, it is not one system—but endless numbers of systems and endless numbers of patterns
that change and change and change and change.
Astrology, numerology, and all these other things are just
trying to tell you that there are sometimes thicker shells
on certain manifestations. All of them, however, must be
broken and transcended and the energy absorbed. It is not
to put you into a pattern. It is to teach you that patterns
exist to be surrendered and the nourishment taken. Within
yourself, understand your ability to be in a deep state of
surrender, to open and allow this force to come in and
work with you. Work with it sensitively—any way that it
wants to come. And if it works fifteen minutes and then
comes in another way, surrender this and go there. Be real-
istic with it, don't be an illusionist chasing something to
the right for fifty years when the thing has shifted fifteen
thousand times already.

Growth has to do with knowing what is giving
nourishment, not having an illusion of what you think it
should be. It is God's will and God's ever-changing energy that we are open toward, not our will. I mean, if you go
to a cow, you can drink the milk, but if you don't watch it,
you might get kicked in very vital areas. And it's the same

way in spiritual work. You can make a pattern, create an illusion, and even assume something, and you will live in that assumption endlessly. Growth has to do with having the conscious ability to detach and attach again and again.

* * *

You have to want tremendously. You have to ask inside and feel your resistance to growing. When you ask to grow and you find that something says no, go inside again and ask and take a breath and ask again. Feel in you this thing that will not move an inch—this thing that wants to stay the way it is. When you are working deeply enough to feel that resistance, then you have provoked something worthwhile inside you. But a human being working without resistance is not different than a cow in a field chewing the same cud over and over and over.

* * *

How do you break down resistance? By opening more. You absorb resistance by expanding. The resistance becomes energy. So, what is pain? Pain is energy under pressure. You keep asking and asking and asking to break down the pressure, and this flow of energy comes in. Working without resistance, however, has nothing to do with accomplishments. It has to do with a certain level of expression, and you stay there endlessly, like two people fighting and living together for fifty years. It has nothing to do with transcending, it has nothing to do with a creative life—it has everything to do with living. It has to do with a pattern. As you grow, you have to continually work and ask and feel the resistance within you build up. Then you know that you are about to expand and grow to a level that you have never been to before.

Instead of fighting, sit there, feel, and say, "I wish to open." Do this fifty thousand times until you have enough respect for yourself that you open. I mean, did you ever see a dog in a house with people around? You say, "Now, puppy, don't do that," and what does the puppy do? He pees right there. But if you really talk from inside with authority, and he knows that you are going to beat him with a piece of paper, he won't do it. Unless you can talk from inside yourself with authority, until this thing inside you knows that you mean business, it is not going to open. Why should it open for a fool? Our permissiveness allows us to be destroyed spiritually. Because you think, "Well, it doesn't want to open today, so I'll wait awhile and ask again, 'Hello, uh, down there, are you going to open?'" You can die with it. Sit there and say, "I absolutely will not accept this." Sit there hour after hour and this thing will finally say, "Why don't you go home to sleep?" You're annoying it, you're provoking it, you're driving it crazy—it will leave. It will leave and you will open. It is easier living with it than driving it out of you, and you only drive it out by asking thousands of times. Thousands of times.

* * *

By opening deeply, your state of being will attract the extraordinary riches that exist. But nobody ever seems to be conscious of it or want it. Instead you all walk around like babes looking in the street. You don't grow by what you are. You grow by how deeply you work because these things do not exist on this level—they're on higher levels. If your state of being is such, you will attract these gifts. They will be given to you because nobody else wants them. It's a competition, in a sense, because you grow by doing what somebody else is not doing. It is not the amount that you work, it is the depth to which you open. It is the amount that you are willing to surrender, and the lack of reservation that you have in your brain of what you think you are willing to give up or what you think you are not willing to give up.

Ultimately, it has nothing to do with you at all. Your mental attitude of who and what you think you are or what you think you will or won't do has absolutely no meaning. Only by opening and deeply surrendering will it take place. This state of being will begin to function because it is an organic and natural process taking place—very much like the ripening of a carrot or a pineapple. By opening inside, you will be attached to higher levels of consciousness and energy. And because most of you are incomplete as human beings, by receiving this energy, your organs, chakras, and muscles become complete. As the energy flows into them, you ripen.

As you ripen, you will have extraordinary realizations, but they are the realizations that take place in a ripe human being, as a ripe carrot or a ripe pineapple is sweet. It doesn't matter what you did or what you are doing in your life. It has nothing to do with that because these things are simple conditions of a moment. By growing and having this more mature, deeply sweet, and nourishing energy, things will change in you because you will have to live with them. And finally, this is what a gift is, this is what energy is—living with it allows you to change. What you say and think has nothing to do with it, because if you had said and thought the right things, you would have grown up a long time ago. Look at the world. It reflects wrong teaching, not right teaching. People are accumulating more and more tension and only a little spirituality because there is no real example.

Walk around. You don't see many people with a great inner life, with a great inner sigh, with a great inner happiness and freedom. And that is what spirituality is supposed to do. It should free you, it should make you deeply happy. Instead, people let their minds run on and get captured in all kinds of stupid ways because one person said this and another said that. It is all secondary to whether you can receive nourishment, assimilate it, and grow. Feel it. Feel the muscles expanding, feel your heart expanding, and take in this nourishment just as a child takes in its mother's milk. Feel these muscles actually growing in you. This growth and maturity is a natural process of development that brings a higher level of spirituality—not the tensions of thinking and getting emotional.

In the same way, a carrot is ripe when it pushes up through the ground. So, as you ripen, you push from one level to another, regardless of the resistance you might have inside. If you open and feel the swell of energy, this thing has to break through. By pushing through the ground and absorbing more and more energy, you have to pop lightly into another level. The best way to grow is to relate with depth, with feeling, with love, and with flow. To criticize, tear apart, and make a mold blocks the energy within you. When you feel this tension, you have to stay open. It means that this carrot is beginning to hit the top of the soil and is just pushing its way through the ground.

If it gets nourishment, it will come through. But usually, when we feel these things, we withdraw—it's too painful. And you never break through.

* * *

*E*very day now I have a lot of resistance, and I must say it is wonderful. People come and say things that would have driven me crazy ten years ago. I find it wonderful that I can really grow. This is what consciousness is about—it's to not destroy your lines of nourishment when you attract things that want to take your nourishment away. It is to love, open, relate to, be responsible for, and still feel the tensions around you. You are moving up against all of these resistances. The higher you move, of course, the more resistances you feel—it's no different than the executive of a large corporation. I mean, nobody bothers the shipping clerk or the guy sweeping the floor. As you get more authority and grow in any kind of position, the responsibilities increase. Growth depends on your ability to not take the tensions personally—or even accept them at all. You don't have to live in a cocktail lounge when you finish your day's work.

CHAPTER 5

You have to understand the difference between tensions and spirituality. Tension is crippling and most of the things you have been miserable about are tensions. There are right tensions, karmic tensions, and bad karmic tensions, which the nourishment coming to you begins to break down. You can't grow spiritually until your muscles and chakras are formed. But they can't open and flower until they ripen; and until then, they can't sustain a flow and give you the kind of service you want. You must understand this. On a physical level, you can become free. But until you can feel your heart and every other chakra open beyond your chest, you are limiting yourself. Your physical body is still more than your spiritual body. Ultimately, your spiritual body has to be more than your physical body.

This is a big factor in what stops people from growing. They want without a foundation, they want without maturity and growth, they want without pain. And you can't do it. There has to be a consistent effort and you have to grow through level after level of development until you feel the muscles. As you breathe, your heart opens and you can feel your energy flowing down to your

sex organs and being refined. You won't be a great eques-
trian after your first half-hour riding lesson. You have to
practice. You have to become one with whatever it is you
are studying. Until you feel from your heart and try to
open from your heart and relate from your heart, until
you try to take a breath and feel open a hundred times a
day, you will never grow. It can't be thirty minutes or
twenty-four hours of superficiality. It must be a complete
surrender and a deep opening.

   Bring your mind inside and ask and ask and ask
until you feel there is nothing left in you—until you are
asking from a state of nothingness, not a state of "somethingness." Ask until you are in a total state of surrender.
Really want from that depth where you are willing to
become nothing, to have a sense of nothingness—not a
sense of "I'm giving up a little more, I'm going a little
deeper." Go on until there is nothing left and you can feel
the void within you. A sharp sense of nothingness—open
so deeply that you can open no more and then take a
breath down. It's like cutting somebody right through the
middle and throwing away both halves. You have no ego
left because you know you are nothing but a vehicle
through which this thing runs. You are nothing. It's like
drilling for water. You dig and dig and dig and dig, and
finally you hit water. It may be at five hundred feet, it may
be at sixty feet, but the longer it takes to dig, the deeper
the well will be. And a sixty-foot well dries up when the
sun comes out, but a five hundred-foot well doesn't. This
work takes time. It took me twenty years during which I
was stark, raving mad.

   You have to understand about wanting a result. Be
grateful that you can work and feel more depth and not

see anything. Because what you are doing is getting deeper and deeper. It means you can get through a lot of past karma. If you hit something at sixty feet, you are getting rid of maybe two past lives. So, if you go down five thousand feet, you will be able to get rid of thousands of lives, tens of thousands of years. That is what you are working for. People who work and say, "Oh, I was an Indian princess last time" and go through a whole routine are ridiculous. We go back and up and sideways and everything else for millions of years. These things are not us today. It is stupid and limiting. It's like a beggar being satisfied with somebody dropping a couple of pennies. From here, you think this or that is a big deal. It is nothing but a cheap gift that you are willing to accept because you don't want to be totally nothing.

Things that people think of as a result are what they accept as a payoff. They say, "I can surrender this" and "It's wrong to do this, but that's okay." What's okay? If this is wrong, and this is a manifestation and that is a manifestation, then everything is a manifestation until you open and don't exist. A sense of nothingness is what you are finally working for. You open and each chakra opens so far that you cease to exist. *It* exists—this state of being that you are working toward. It is a state of serving and you become a servant. You are nothing. This thing just comes through, comes through, comes through. You take the dirty rags after you have cleaned all you can and go to sleep, and you have to wash them out while you are sleeping to wake up to work again. It is difficult but it certainly saves you from ever being locked in with yourself and your own image.

* * *

*T*ry to understand what I mean by opening deeper and deeper and really asking. Take a breath and when this thing opens, feel your nothingness. Feel it—feel the magnificence of this love that comes through you. You are fortunate to have it touch you for as long as it flows through you. It means, however, that you have to continually break down everything you do. The things you do during the day are just tests of your doubts. These things during the day are manifestations not to be attached to. Whether you think it is important or unreal, it is all the same garbage. It doesn't matter how the energy comes wrapped. If you just remember the content and surrender to it, you can open the package and take out the content. And don't worry about it. You can't put a value on it because you don't know what is deep and what is important. It all flows like many streams into the same river and goes into a reservoir. Your work is to allow this energy to come through you, to not judge it, to not in any way understand. That is your true function.

* * *

*Y*ou have to let things go. As things come, that's when you can make a choice. You say, "No, not this again," or you wait for the next bump. If you wait for the next bump, you can go in a different direction and change your pattern. You have a choice with the attraction; with what falls away, you have no choice. With what changes, you have no choice because what is changing expresses God's will. It's the changing that does it. If you love somebody, your love carries them to other levels and gives them the right to move on. We think that when we love people, they have to be constant or tied. It's not true. Loving is detachment and nourishment and moving. You move here, somebody moves there; you move there, somebody moves here. If you have consciousness and want to serve these people, change and serve them. Go in their direction. This is really what it's all about—that the weaker, dependent person follows. That is why, in Biblical times, a man was considered stronger, and the woman followed him. Today, if there is such a thing as a follower, it is manifested by the man and the woman growing together, and one saying, "I'm stronger than you." And either one may follow. It is strength and consciousness and a higher need for nourishment that should not be expressed as fighting. The only way people can stay together harmoniously is by compromising direction because of attraction and a need for nourishment.

* * *

I got a call today from somebody who I love and respect. He is the American head of the Zen movement on the West Coast. He is an extraordinary man and one of the greatest and humblest human beings I have ever met. And he is very aware of his responsibilities. I saw him when I was last out in California. And while I have never been to his place at Big Sur and certainly am not involved in Zen Buddhism, I have seen some remarkable people with him.

I was going out to California and told his people in San Francisco to notify him that I would come and pay my respects to him. The first night I was in San Francisco, before I could go to him, he came to me and brought six or eight people. I was already seated when he arrived, and he sat on the floor. If I had known he was coming, I would have had enough seats for them. But he didn't require it, there was nothing in him that wanted. It made you want to kiss his feet. It was a tribute to him.

Then I went to see him. He told me he was going to light incense in front of his Buddha and bow three times—meaning, I could bow or not bow. We were in his temple, he was in charge, but he gave me the right to not follow the ritual. For me, it was wonderful. I bowed and did everything else he did because I would not bring down the level of experience for anyone else.

This is what freedom should be—that you are given choices. Being open to expand, to change, to encompass doesn't take away from a situation. It makes the situation more. To grow, it is very important to learn this. You should always bring up the level of the people around you. Real growth should bring up your mother and father and your brothers and sisters and everybody whose lives touch yours.

* * *

There are people who come into our lives who cut the wires, who cut off the flow of water, who destroy the things that are vital to our growth. It is always a sign of somebody who wants control. They start separating you from your root system and from that which gives you your fuel or energy. This is what destroys a lot of marriages—a wife doesn't like her husband travelling, she doesn't like his family, she doesn't like this, and she doesn't like him. If you take away the flow of energy that has created a person, you must be able to replace it. And if you can't, then you certainly shouldn't take it away.

If people eliminate the attachments that you use to draw energy, you are left completely vulnerable. In your own living, if you find that you attract something better, something deeper, then the other will automatically fall away as you grow. In a tree, the bottom leaves turn brown and little shoots grow out the top. Unless you see growth, don't surrender attachment. Attachment falls away because of growth, not because of will. It is a natural, organic process of growing, but we always want to go through and trim the tree and do this and do a million other things. And before we know it, we put the tree into a state of shock. It can't assimilate anything.

You can't shock something when the roots are small. The time to trim a tree is in the winter, when it is dormant. You trim away the deadness so that life can come, not trim away the life and leave the deadness. It is to become conscious of what increases this flow—what is you, what you need, not what you want. So many times, what you want is lots of fertilizer—and that will burn out your root system. It is the same thing in a relationship when you start by loving someone passionately. God and nature take care of that in a couple of weeks. Otherwise, you would never be able to get up in the morning—you would be falling on your face.

CHAPTER 6

We can go on and on about people who vilify blacks or Jews or Italians. They will destroy a race or culture based on some stupid experience they had or some propaganda they heard. It is the nature of people to do this. We get caught in our minds and become completely limited by past experience, by the way we were raised, without the capacity to separate our emotions or ideas and find in things that which is good. If we see in a box of tomatoes one that is rotten, we throw the whole thing away. We discard much of the depth of our lives by fixating on something superficial that we see. We limit everybody, and we certainly limit ourselves.

In spirituality, this is more prevalent than anywhere else because the process of growing is based on dying—the destruction of one thing to give life to something else. The thing that occurs with people is endless complaining and whining and feeling only that which is dying and not that which is coming to life. Become aware that to grow we have to be able to separate it from the whole. These expressions are worthless and have nothing to do with attaining what is important. Going forward and paying a price is part of our consciousness. It is our reality and the only way we can expect to attain our objective.

* * *

As we work, we feel pain, we feel tensions, we feel confusion. We have to say, "Fine, what's the confusion?" We are going through this morass of stuff, we are going through this dusty hallway where we have stored so much of our garbage from today and from years and even lifetimes past. It has to be confusing. How can you make order out of the chaos that is the accumulation of thousands of years—or maybe thousands of lifetimes. We think that when we work spiritually we are in contact with reality. But we are no more in contact with reality than a person in an insane asylum is in contact with reality. We are beginning to mix up levels. We are doing the one thing that is guaranteed to confuse us. We are trying to become more rational on our ordinary physical levels while, at the same time, reaching to another level. We are doing two things at once. While trying to solidify one level, we are disturbing the level above it. This is why so much difficulty and confusion arise.

Growth is always that. As we reinforce one thing, we destroy another. This is the symbolism of the Hindu deity Shiva—the destroyer and the giver of life. These things happen simultaneously. Only a fool can study spiritually and feel this lightness, this joy, this sweetness all of the time. These should be there in spite of the level that is dying, in spite of that which is being destroyed. Our consciousness should become broad enough to encompass this lesser existence that is going away and we should relate to this higher existence that we are working toward. Unless we identify with this rebirth, it will never take place. Instead, all of our energy will be absorbed into this descending force instead of into the transcending force. And this is where transcending is essential. We say, "I feel this thing in me."

And, believe me, I feel the pain. Daily this energy is coming and tearing me up, but it is tearing out a level that allows me to climb to a higher level. I don't like it and I can't say that I get used to it. It goes on for a long, long time. I want to explain it so that when you encounter this thing, you will understand it. It does not mean you are not working well. It means you are working the best way any human being can work. When you feel Buddha in heaven and yourself floating over everything, it just means that you are in the bus station waiting for the next bus. Nothing is accomplished waiting for the next bus. If you want to stay in the bus station for the rest of your life, it's all right with me. But it doesn't represent growing and moving along the path. It represents being retired, and you might as well go down to Florida and sit on a bench. At least you will be in the sun with the other old people.

To grow is to have the courage to say, "Fine, I have attained something wonderful because I did this work consciously. I can face the issues of my life. I can consciously allow this thing or that thing to break up because I believe and I understand that only by surrendering and allowing this thing to grind itself away can I become free." The alternative is to sit there, whistle away, and tell people how great you are and how fantastic this thing is that you attained. And nothing is worse in this world than being anticlimactic to your own growth.

* * *

The whole process of growth is understanding what you are involving yourself in. Technically, you can't succeed in anything unless you understand what you are building. You don't know what you have to put into it, you don't know the strain or stress, and you have no idea of your direction. People sign up on many kinds of trips other than spiritual trips, and crap out because they didn't bring along the right equipment. If you are going on a jaunt in the English countryside, you don't wear high heels. You dress in a sensible way. Well, the same thing applies to our work. You have to be comfortable. You have to be prepared for the kind of longevity that requires an extraordinary amount of endurance and simplicity. This is because the psychodrama that will be attracted by your growth will be unbelievable—and because as energy rises, it attracts. You don't have to do anything. You can sit down and do your work and grow, and it will bring you more than you can possibly conceive of. Energy attracts. Sitting quietly attracts a different kind of situation. But working and evolving and growing and expanding generate a great deal of energy. If inside you don't have a simple base and a sense of what you really want in your life, you will never be able to survive.

This kind of survival yoga has to do with endless growing. You have to ask deeply and open deeply so that this feeling of infinity and endless work is possible. It is not an ego development or a satisfaction in an external sense. That will come, because everything will be given to a human being who tries to grow and grow and grow. The rewards come, the temptations come, and everything else comes along with it. There will be infinite stages of ego-mania when you think you are anything from the Buddha or Jesus Christ to some other creature that lived at another point in time. All of these things represent certain levels of energy under certain types of tension and pressure. The greater the pressure, the more you feel you are something. As you become more secure, your sense of nothingness will grow and your capacity to surrender and become freer will express itself in your sense of nothingness.

You will get to an advanced stage where you open within yourself and feel this energy—and I mean an energy that surpasses the immediate energy around you, this six or twelve inches of electricity that emanates from you and into you. You get beyond that. Once you open the chakras beyond the immediate field of your own existence, you begin to reach into space and time. And that's really where the most wonderful part of spirituality begins. Instead of being stuck in an off-Broadway production of "Porgy and Bess," you enter the big time. You really open, and there's a cast of thousands, and you are right in the middle. It's beautiful. You begin to see past lives, you begin to experience all these magnificent things. But you have to be sure that they throw you out after the performance. Because if you get stuck at that stage, baby, you will never get off the boards. You will be bouncing around doing the same number for the next six thousand years.

What you are attracting is another kind of manifestation, but in more magnificence. It has its beautiful moments, but it is a re-run of something you did a long time ago. These spiritual re-runs are when we reach out beyond ourselves, when these chakras open, and the magnificence that every human being contains is expressed by the freedom of reaching beyond this confined area of the physical self. You find people of five thousand years ago, and three thousand years ago, and ten and twenty thousand years ago. You look at them and not only feel something, but you say, "Ah, you were..." You know who they were; you feel it. You don't have to express it in too many words because this thing will be expressed in energy, and from them to you the content of these past relationships and these past lifetimes flows. Within this are found the real riches of spirituality. You are milking the universe and taking from it the structural content of the energy of many past ages. To grow and be free is to reach back into time and space, make these contacts, and take those energies. That is finally what frees you.

* * *

Einstein's theory of relativity expressed itself this way. And yoga is this. We free ourselves to become one, one, one, one, one, one, one over a million years. It is unbelievable. And those who feel Buddhist or Hindu or Jewish or Christian or whatever are only tapping one small area of their past existences. To begin to feel and express it in very tangible terms is what we should be working for. Begin to taste the limitlessness of it, the freedom, the sweetness, the glory of it and, more than anything else, the nothingness of it. We begin to understand that this thing has in this expression the true depth of nothingness, which is everything.

We should have within us the consciousness to reach for this as we surrender the tensions of today. Your life only expresses this limitation because your mind is locked behind endless walls of this moment in which you have stored all past lives. Take a breath and open and feel the swing go on and on and on. These chakras dare to go beyond this little periphery of your limited mind. So that when you do meet people, you can feel the love and the depth you once had with them—that was there and will always be there. It will not be lost regardless of whether they are here or somewhere else. Your relationship with them is not because of a student's proximity to a teacher or of a friend's to a friend. Rather, it is part of the endlessness that is and always will be there. The loving feeling you have with them will always be there.

A man like Nityananda had that to offer. This man was a void of energy. There was no limitation in him. It was extraordinary. Looking at that black mask sitting there, you would say "What is it?" It was nothing and it was everything. It was extraordinary. Energy poured out of him and poured into anyone who wanted. I didn't know who he was or what he was, and this man poured from himself into the atmosphere, opening something in me. This is something you must understand. It is not your relationship to me, it is your relationship to yourself that allows you to take what I have. And what I have is what he had because he is in me. You can take. Whether or not you like me is of no consequence. Open and take this. It will give you what I received and what hundreds of thousands of people received.

This is not a thing of the mind. It is not a thing of emotions or limitations. It is a very practical, real thing that you can take in because you wish for something beyond this limited experience of fifty or a hundred years. Your mind and your sitting there in your thickness represents your inability to open because you are scared out of your wits. You haven't the guts for it, number one, and you haven't received in your life the nourishment that qualifies you to open. You haven't made the effort. Any one of these things will disqualify you. So sit and really ask for it, keep your attention inside and start opening. Just doing that will allow more to come inside you. You will attract more and expand more.

* * *

*T*here is only one reason not to do—because you don't have the concept and the guts to want to live. You need to justify your life as a loser, you have security only in being a loser, and you want to sit and feel sorry for yourself from now on. Whatever you are in your life has no consequence. And to recognize this is not an act of intelligence, it is not an act of emotion, it is not even an act of spirituality. It is the act of somebody looking and seeing a pile of garbage and being able to say, "I don't want to sit with that." Slowly, you bring your mind inside and start to open and allow this thing to flush out of you. It is as simple as pulling the chain on a toilet. Trying to make it complicated and finding reasons that have to do with the thickness of the mind will not make this move. I have seen a child who would almost let his fingers be broken before he would give up something picked up in the gutter, or a dog that would choke before giving up a bone found in the street.

Only an animal allows itself to live choking on this filth that it picks up. It is dropped easily by just saying, "I don't want that, and I won't be limited by that, and I want to open beyond my physical self, and I want to experience." Just sit there and keep your attention inside, take a breath and this thing will open. Period. Nothing profound, nothing magical about it. When you push the button for the sixth floor, it goes to the sixth floor. You have to understand this as a simple thing. You have to find within yourself that which knows it can do it. Being here proves that you know it can be. To allow yourself to not do certainly will not become a game between me and you. I am not going to wrestle with you over that bone in your throat. If you want it there, you can choke as far as I am concerned. I am not going to give you my energy to play a game. It is a simple thing. If you want to live with it, then you live with it. But I don't want to live with it and I refuse to accept anyone around me who will live with it.

If you open, this will flow into you and you will become free and attract other people that you need. You will be nourished and you will grow and you will begin to understand through your own experience. But this thing cannot be explained—it must be lived.

* * *

We are continually dying and being reborn. It's a matter of going from one level to another. When you can't grow on your present level anymore, you have to move on. You have to lift yourself consciously to a new level through your own will and stay there. Stay there. You will watch everything try to pull you down while you go up again. It doesn't mean you have to change your patterns, just refine or detach from them a little bit. It is like a prize fighter who gets pneumonia and is weak and filled with drugs. He can't fight, right? So he goes and dries out. He goes away for a couple of months, then he gets back into training so that he can fight.

We have to know when to retire from this fight. It is like having someone very strong and negative next to you. You can fight every day but it will do no good.

However, if you shut your mouth for three months and get quiet, not only will you drive him crazy, you will have the energy to go beyond the entire affair. You will go to a higher level. Your logic will knock him out. You will not only have the capacity to sustain yourself, you will have enough energy to endure and bludgeon him if necessary. It is because we always fight the same battles in the same way, we completely bleed out the energy we need to transcend the situation.

* * *

I am going through something now. I know that something in me is dying, and I am very grateful for it. And so, I sit quietly and have thirty-two cups of tea in the store. I try to read a murder mystery and stay as easy as I can. And very open, to allow it to die. I don't want to feed energy into the death. This thing is dying, and from the floor to the ceiling I feel terrible. I really feel terrible. But on the next floor there is something beginning to come to life. I feel grateful enough and conscious enough to allow that new life to come into being even if I can't see it. I may see it a day or a week from now. And I know when I feel like this that there is no reason in the world for me to feel badly—because my life is wonderful. I am very grateful. When there is no logic for something, the only reason is that something in you is trying to die—and you try to rationalize something that is not rational. You will fight it and ask that it be made rational, but the only way to make it rational is to raise it to a higher level. Then, at least, you can benefit from that level. So attach on that level, begin to make friends on that level, and the other slowly dies away.

* * *

To open, you just have to sit down and do it. It is like the two thieves meeting on Avenue Y.

One of them asks, "How d'ya do today?"

The other replies, "I took two hundred dollars. What d'ya do?"

"I did five thousand dollars."

"Wow, where?"

"I went up to 56th Street and Park Avenue."

Right . . . If you stay in your own neighborhood, the pickings are pretty lousy because it has been picked over. It is a poor neighborhood. You already have absorbed and juiced it. The tensions in you have absorbed it. Why should you keep opening in the same place? Move into a new neighborhood. Open and go out and out and out and out and out. It is much better to open the heart chakra and forget about the rest of them for the time being. At least they will come back with a lot of delicacies, nourishment, new feelings, new energy. It will be very, very exciting. Feel the nothingness of this extraordinary consciousness and this extraordinary energy. When you have a lousy day, you are filled with yourself. When it is an extraordinary day, you are filled with the magnificence of nothingness. If the sunshine is there and the sunset is there, do you understand? You are so open that every-thing is there—and that means that you are not there. You've gone into the beyond.

* * *

As long as you are dying here, go out and start building on the next level. If you are dying here and you

are coming to life there, do something there. Change a pattern in yourself. Open to somebody or something in a different way that represents being freer, being more open,
being more extraordinary. You have to raise your level of
expression and consciousness.

Nothing matters if you are finished. Do you
understand? Maybe you like marzipan and you don't like
chocolate, maybe you like chocolate and you don't like
something else. It doesn't matter. There is no reason to
measure or judge anything else. It's just another world.
But I don't want to be in a world. I want to be in a state of
nothingness. I don't care and I can open to the content that
flows and nourishes me. Period. If it doesn't flow and
nourish me, it will not be because I haven't opened to it. I
will have opened to it.

The other day, a woman brought someone to my
store who ordinarily would not be the kind of person I
would want to relate to. But I am not relating to a person—I am relating to a symbol, and a person is a symbol.
So, I surrendered in myself and opened and found something that for me was an opportunity to grow, and I had a
wonderful couple of hours. I would much rather make an
effort to surrender and grow into a different level and
dimension of relationship—not be restricted by patterns
or types or races or groups. It is stupid. Why should anything stop us from opening and sharing the nourishment
that another human being has to give? Because we like
this. Maybe I like blond-haired people and this one likes
that one, and that one likes this one. It is so stupid. It is
just a label. If I work twice with you, then you are getting
twice as much for your money. What's the difference? The
packaging should have nothing to do with the content.

And we all look at packaging. We have no capacity to surrender, open, take the content, and be grateful for that. And this is all we represent to each other. When you say, "Well, I love this kind of person," but every time you go home, your guts are hanging out and your emotions are wrecked. What does it mean? It means that you have a taste for something that gives you the hives and worse. You have to begin to realize that this kind of psychic feeding is not for you. You need a good doctor to say, "Don't associate with these people, associate with those people." You have to be intelligent about what feeds you and what doesn't feed you, and then know which direction to take. But your mind keeps going there because, you know, if he is a Harvard graduate, then he must be a great person. Stupid. I have had more than one case of indigestion from Harvard graduates—they don't all go down that easily. You have to become aware in your life of what your chemistry can take. It doesn't mean that it is permanent, it just means that at this moment you can't afford it. You can't afford to continually repeat the same pattern endlessly, endlessly, by going to the same bar and picking up somebody and getting hit over the head with a log. Even a rat in a cage, after it gets hit a couple of times, stops going back. But we repeat our karma worse than any rat in a cage.

The thing is, we are repeating this pattern routine over and over. Getting hit over the head and going back again. We have to become aware of what we need and what needs us, and see if we can live with it happily and gracefully.

CHAPTER 7

Spirituality is not a thing of the mind. It is something you have to absorb, digest, and balance because there is nothing there to discuss.

Many times students will come, and I will look at them and see whatever they are. Suddenly, something will walk out of them, something will walk out of me, and this thing will take place in the middle of the room. It is the *shakti*—the marriage of my energy and their energy. It is extraordinary. Then we see it on a higher level and begin to experience where we are with them and what we know of them. We begin to understand that in other people we have parts of ourselves that must be freed.

We always have a tendency toward that which goes away or rejects us to put a wall around it and call it dead. This is common in primitive societies—in Italy, if somebody does something unacceptable, a curse is put on him, and that person no longer exists. A family will separate and relatives will never talk to each other again. This kind of mentality cannot break down a wall, so it builds more and more and more. This exists in a primitive society where the people over the hill are your mortal enemies.

Spiritually, we do exactly the opposite. We break down and break down and break down, and finally there are no more walls. When there are no walls, we can rise to a higher level. How can anything express God or religion or anything creative when it builds walls to defend itself? There is no need.

* * *

I woke up the other morning after a funny experience. I heard something saying, "How can you, being what you are, attain this?" And the answer came, "Well, if I, being what I am, could be what I am by working so hard, imagine what you could be if you worked as hard."

It comes only from working. It doesn't matter what you are or who you are, it matters what you do and how hard you work. The classic example is the Chinese laundryman who comes to the city, washes and irons shirts all day long, saves up his money, and goes home and gets a position in his own village. Or people who come here from Puerto Rico, work five or ten years, go back to the mountains, and set up a little business. I know several who have created wonderful lives for themselves.

We finally have to realize that we get by doing. Not by talking, not by hating other people, not by building walls and defending ourselves, but by expanding and doing. You feel this thing, this gift, this magnificence. And magnificence is always an expression of God—it is more and we are nothing. We see our nothingness by feeling this magnificence.

Spiritual growth has to do with feeling—not with the mind. You grow and you feel the change—like a caterpillar changing into a butterfly. You look at somebody, you feel something, you don't have to limit it. You know something is taking place. You open more and begin to see that it is different. You begin to open a little more and see that it is another level of existence. By reaching toward that, you keep growing.

* * *

The real test is always the people you work with. Instead of feeling superior, raise their levels. Work to break yourself down. Free yourself to feel more in them. A superior person makes a superior effort. Break yourself open and nourish the people in your life. Raise them up by giving them from yourself. Feed them from your own being. Break yourself down. If you can't find something good in them, work and work and work and nourish them until something opens, and then work from that. Keep that alive and it grows. Something grows.

We look for things that can destroy our connections with people because we don't want them. We don't have the intelligence to keep connected, so we listen to gossip and search for what is wrong. We eat the pits and throw away the food. It is ridiculous. You have to take nourishment, feed the situation, love, give, and expand. Only then will these tensions disappear. Keep putting into the situation and this wall has to fall down. Because the situation grows and grows, this tension has to crumble. It grows and grows and another wall falls. But either you are feeding tensions or you are nourishing a person in the situation.

So, when you see the tension of a situation, say, "No, I don't want to see this. It only represents a shell. Instead I will reach inside and nourish the situation." And the best way to break down tension is to nourish the inner being of the person and the situation. Love that and feel the need that is there. Whatever is crushed only represents the external limitation. By breaking down your shell, you grow strong.

* * *

Student: A person I knew and hadn't seen for a year came to see me, and she was talking and driving me crazy. And I didn't know what to do. I finally said, "Well, I hope you are all right," and just pushed the situation away.

Rudi: No, you were stupid because you let her talk to you from what's there. You didn't rise above the situation. You didn't make the effort to transcend yourself because you didn't feel she was worth it. Your lack of respect for her kept you in a place where she was throwing garbage at you. And by staying there, you deserved it.

That's why people blast you. And I have gotten caught like that many times in my life, particularly when I am tired. Somebody will walk into the store, act like an animal, and kick things around. If I come down to that level to respond, the person will throw dirt in my face every time. And there is no defense because I shouldn't be there. If a person acts like a dog, you should rise to a higher level. In your case, this woman will realize that there is nobody there for her to talk to—and she will leave.

* * *

An oyster opens when you heat it. And all things ripen with time and chemistry. In spiritual work, you are getting your chemistry together.

You can program yourself before you go to sleep. You can go to sleep open. You can say, "Look, I want to grow inside. I want to gather a great deal of energy. I want to live to grow and transcend myself." Then you will have that kind of rest and take in that kind of energy.

Consciously separate yourself from your body. You can do that. Rise up and let your body fall down. You don't have to carry it with you for that. It's like when you take out the garbage, you don't take along the refrigerator and the stove. So, when sending up your wish to grow, you don't have to take along your body. You say, "Let that go up" and your body will sleep like a log. You are carrying with you all the equipment you need.

* * *

In the beginning, the way to move yourself to the first level of doing is to fill yourself with something else. Get rid of yourself by replacing "you" with a stuffing. This stuffing has to do with doing your spiritual work, surrendering "you," being more attached. You can be more attached to me, more attached to the ashram, more attached to your husband, more attached to all these things. Just fill yourself with attachments.

What happens when you are filled with attachments is that you are not filled with yourself. Eventually, these attachments will leave you because life wants it that way. And when situations and relationships are ripped out of you, you can get filled with God. People who have never been attached, who have never had their guts ripped out, are only filled with themselves—it is ego.

Unconsciously, by not being ripped open, you haven't allowed yourself to attract that which can rip you out. And it is essential. You are protecting yourself. "No one is *not* going to meet me at the movies again. No one is *not* going to pick me up. No one is going to do *it* to me." This self-protectiveness is what destroys us. If we don't allow ourselves to be pulled apart, somebody or some situation has to come along to do it.

In our lives, we have to be plucked—just like a chicken. And then we're clean. We get emptied by valuing, by wanting, by being intense with a lot of things. If you have done a good job in your life, it is wonderful. You are very fortunate. Otherwise, you are filled with yourself and later in life something will come in and start to attach itself inside and grow. It wants to pull you, and you have all these attachments you can't afford—thirty-two children all college age. You can't afford to be disrupted, and you go through life without having your guts ripped out.

This is the one level of existence in which, once it goes, you get filled with spirituality. When you empty out, you are filled with God. There are three levels of stuffing in our existence: first, we are filled with "us," then we are filled with "it." When "it" goes, we have our spirituality.

In a sense, you get filled with me if you have nothing else to fill you. It's a cheap stuffing that eventually you have to have pulled out for you to have your liberation—because I am not a substitute for God. I am a temporary filling. A teacher is and should only be that. That is why if you really want realization, use everything to fill you and then consciously surrender it all. You always separate, or should separate, a person from a teacher at a particular point. It is necessary.

It isn't easy for me—but it makes for respect, it makes for reality, and it makes for equality. If you really want respect, you have to make a person your equal, not your servant.

CHAPTER 8

*C*hakras don't open in a day, or in a week, or even in a year for some people. How can they? You have been dead in your heart for five thousand years and in your solar plexus for twenty thousand years.

Practitioners of Zen Buddhism grunt from their bellies like gorillas. These chakras have taken millions of years to evolve—not two thousand years or even ten thousand years. These are ancient energy centers that originally belonged to different beings. The throat chakra was the gills of a fish. The heart was a bird. The solar plexus was a gorilla. And the base of the spine was a dinosaur—the tail of a prehistoric beast with the brain of a man, which is why it is so difficult.

These things that everyone assumes are equal were equal only in conception and inception. They are millions of years old. And so, interestingly, we think according to Darwin's theory or some other theory that Man was a fish or a baboon. In fact, Man was everything, and we limit ourselves in thinking that it was this or that. It is not this or that—it is this *and* that and that and that and that. We are always more than we can believe. Always. Much more. Much more vast and much deeper. I feel this at the base of my spine, as a matter of fact. It is like a tail five blocks long that can go bang, bang, bang, and I have tremendous energy. Realize that when you are opening a chakra so enormous it could not possibly open in a day. When you begin to stretch your mind to realize how extraordinary and deep these things are, you become grateful for feeling anything. You are actually reaching into time and space. These chakras exist in time and space—not in your physical body. You are trying to connect with an energy that is millions of years old.

So, what is yoga? What is anything? It's tiny, like measuring a billion miles with a ruler. You say, "Here's a billion miles," and we look at a twelve-inch ruler. We measure ourselves and our own lives on this infinitely small scale, and since we have the universe in this twelve inches, that anything works is a miracle. It is so unbelievably big, and we are so encrusted with a billion years of crud. These things are deeply latent in people. And instead of opening, what they do is hate this one because he is one thing, and that one because he is something else.

* * *

You have to work with consciousness. You have to open and digest. As the energy comes in, feel it flowing, breathe—do the double- or single-breath exercise as you need. Maybe five times in a half hour. Every time you finish the breathing exercise, you have taken in a quantity of your energy, my energy, and God's energy. And then it should be absorbed. To become yours, it should be absorbed and digested and transcended. Otherwise it is coming in and going out, coming in and going out. Glunk, it all goes out again, you do the same thing over, and a negligible amount is digested. Consciously belch yourself by opening, transcending, and allowing your muscles to absorb the energy and expand. That energy stays within you. Because you have expanded and transcended, the energy is absorbed and your chakras grow. They grow because they suck this energy deeply into their individual root systems and use it to expand.

* * *

*D*o you ever take a breath while you are working and feel yourself moving up? You feel an expansion or a stretching. This means the energy is coming into the chakra. Put your hands together like this: the base of each palm touching and the fingers spread apart and out. Now feel energy in the middle of your palms. Feel it, and then move the tips of your fingers very, very slightly. Do you feel the energy going through your fingers? Move your fingers a little more. Feel the energy in your fingers, feel the energy in your palms. Now move your fingers a little more. The energy goes right down into your wrists. It's like the base of a flower. And that is what you should feel in the chakras. You are making a whole—you are taking two halves and making a whole. You are making a flower out of your hands. The minute you do it, you have psychically created a living plant that can draw in energy, and you feel this thing move. You should feel this in your heart—that the energy is sucked into the outside of the heart muscles, is drawn into the core, and expands from the base of the core. It is remarkable.

* * *

Yesterday something wonderful happened. I realized that as this year progresses, a lot of things will come out for me and I will grow. I will become a more known quantity and for the first time in my life I will encounter prejudice because, in growing, I will provoke unsure people. I thought of it yesterday for the first time and it was very funny—people will hate me for specific reasons. They will say, "Oh, he's Jewish, and he's this, and he's that," and I've never had this in my life. I suddenly sat there thinking, "My God, I'm on the brink of a whole new experience." It doesn't bother me. What does it matter? They will reject me for one reason or another because what people like or don't like has to do only with their need to protect themselves. So when someone says, "I won't take from you because of this or that," it is not me—it is that person. That person has resistance and has to label something. And we always label the things we fear with something that can stop us from taking.

It's the same way we take milk from a cow. If, in your curiosity about a cow, you lift his tail and look up the behind, you are going to see shit. This is true of everything and everybody. Everything that gives nourishment also has a mechanism that makes garbage. Well, we are not busy in life classifying garbage. We should be busy in life taking nourishment. So either you are looking up the behind of every domestic animal that lived, which makes you an expert on shit, or you receive nourishment from everything, which makes you grow. Most people are experts on shit.

* * *

Once in India, I was treated in a violent way that was driving me crazy. And so I asked Swami Venkateshananda, whom I will love forever, about it. He said, "I can't tell you one thing or another. I can only ask you, 'Are you above it?'" It was incredible. I went "Oh . . ." and rose right above it. Why analyze what was going on; there was nothing to analyze. If I could rise above it, I could walk away from it. But by being involved with it, I became part of it. If I resented it, I hated it, it was cruel, it was stupid, it was this, it was that—and all the talking in the world would do nothing but feed it—but when I surrendered it and rose above it, I was free.

The problem is finding something on the level on which it exists. You can never stand it because you become part of it. Simply detach from it and say, "I wish to surrender and not be on that level." You detach by taking a deep breath and opening, which detaches your energy from that connection, allowing you to separate and rise above it. You are free. Only after being free of something for six months can you realize what it was and that it's over. It becomes history. But fighting anything face to face is illusionary because you are not objective, you are not detached, you are not above it. You will never understand it with the mind. You have to really surrender, do your breathing exercise, feel yourself open, and rise above it. Then, look and see.

It's the same as having lousy friends—people who keep you up all night, eating your energy and spitting it in your face. You may get mad at them, but you will be there forever because you are attached to it. But if you send

them home at ten o'clock at night, you can go to sleep and
wake up in the morning with the energy to be above the
situation a little more each day. In four weeks, you won't
know them or they will change. How can they respect
you, anyway, if you are there with them. It never will
work because you never will find an answer on the level
of the problem. Consciousness is the ability to detach and
feel yourself rise above it—and most of the time we don't
want to rise above it because we would rather fight. We
express our energy on that level because we want to stay
on that level. Our security is on that level. When we
detach, we save our energy and free ourselves to become
real human beings.

* * *

When you consciously draw in the electrical
field around you through the head, the brain, down the
front, in a sense you wash through your own life force and
energy, shake out all negative psychic tensions, and
stretch. As you open more and more and more, you feel
life force rise up your spine to the top of your head. You
really are stretching and transcending yourself—like
going from the first floor to the second floor. And when
you go to the third floor, what happens? As you go higher,
this weight automatically drops off like a skin being shed
or a balloon losing ballast.

When you are up in a balloon and want to go
higher, you drop a couple of sandbags. To rise, you have
to drop off weight; you have to consciously visualize it.
You are opening, expanding, and taking in more energy.
Taking in more energy is like putting more gas in the bal-

loon. As you take in more energy, feel yourself consciously rise and then drop. As you rise, you should also be
dropping—and doing these two things consciously. You
are taking in more energy, opening more and more and
more. You feel the muscles take in more energy. You feel
the energy enter the core of each chakra and then collec-
tively flow through your sex organs and up your spinal
column to the top of your head. You go up and then surrender negative psychic tensions. Rising allows you to
drop some of this weight consciously. Otherwise, the
weight is there and you return to the same level. Your
molecular structure stays the same. Whenever you rise,
you consciously have to drop some of these things so they
can't reform again. Let this psychic glue drop through
your fingers and say, "I want to drop all the negative psychic tensions not necessary for my spiritual growth." This
breaks the molecular pattern because you are dropping
some of the heavier tensions.

* * *

We talk about somebody being an instrument of
the flow because the inner tube through which the spiritual force flows can grow and expand. It only expands as
you grow spiritually and your state of nothingness—not
your state of somethingness—expands. You are consciously bringing this state of nothingness inside your life force
and expanding it and refining the energy when it rises to
the top of your head. It then descends through the chakras
again, making them finer and more elastic. This is the process of bringing in energy and refining it. Either you do
this every day or you become some kind of idiot beating

your brain against the ground wanting things that are not possible. We only get things by attracting them through our own energy—and everything in life is an attraction. Your energy rises, it expands, you attract. It goes up another level, you expand, you attract, you absorb more energy, you go up, you expand, you take in more energy, you absorb it, you go up. It is a process of eating. As human beings, we are either expanding and contracting; consuming energy, digesting it, and refining it; or we are stuck for life on the same level.

* * *

*P*eople who grow are the ones who change a little bit every day. While those who grow keep raising and changing their levels, people with strong egos always assume they know what to do. This assumption, this acceptance of yourself in a stable way, doesn't represent stability—it represents crystallization. As energy in the atmosphere is ever-changing, so a human being should be ever-changing. You should be growing, expanding, feeling the flow of this force going through you. You have to be able to take a breath one day and feel your life force come down from the middle of your head into your throat, through your heart, and all the way down to your sex organs and up your spinal column. You have to feel all day long at will that you are a living, breathing, functioning, expanding human being and recognize what is required inside.

I know that because of the enormous opening that came from my birthday ten days ago, I have to live above a great many tensions. I absolutely cannot afford an involvement with people on certain levels and I can't afford certain kinds of emotions. So I went to my store and said inside myself, "Look, I don't care." I let myself, in a sense, speak to God and said, "Please, I will surrender my business and anything else not to return to the same level." I have to save my energy to nourish this thing that is trying to grow. And I went a little higher and became a little lighter in myself, and then, lo and behold, I did business from that level. I did not have to extend myself to do it. I simply stayed on a higher level and allowed a lot to take place.

In other words, we don't have to become material to do material acts. We don't have to become physical to do physical acts. We can consciously stay above the level we are performing on. And if we stay above, then what happens? The act is finished, the energy rises to fill the void between you and where the act took place, and because of this attachment you drain energy out of a situation that ordinarily you would feed. It is the same if you sat with someone who was very argumentative. You say inside, "I will not fight with her, regardless of what happens, I will respect her, I will try to nourish her, I will try to see her side of it. I really will try to serve her." You tell yourself strongly the attitude that you will maintain so that when the person comes, you really are above the situation and can detach yourself from the ordinary level of that relationship. You stay there and as you feel yourself being pulled down, you say, "No, I won't judge her, I really will stay here." You open your heart to fill the void between where you would be emotionally and mentally with consciousness.

The separation and detachment that you are allowing yourself to live with must be filled—and it can only be filled with consciousness. Consciousness is a vacuum because of its outstretched energy, and it is so light that it allows the flow from that person to come to you. And your flow can go to her because it is not filled with the heaviness of thinking, of prejudice, of knowing. So, in a sense, you are making a filter between yourself and the other person that allows a purification, a refinement in attitude and feeling, to take place. You are not judging or prejudging her. You force yourself to rise above the situation and fill the space between with a consciousness that allows this flow to come.

* * *

*F*or many reasons, I just accepted someone who is going to be a difficult student. This person is physically very sick, mentally very disturbed, and a lot of other things. In the whole structure of this person, however, I can see a few very precious diamonds. When you consciously start off with people who are handicapped, you never have the right to oppress them with their conditions. You can say, all right, I know they lack certain things, so you can't suddenly say, "Look, you're crippled." You knew they were crippled, you took them with that condition. So you build into yourself a detachment between yourself and them and fill this void with a compassion, an understanding, a commitment higher in nature than you ordinarily have with another person. It is a chance to do something extraordinary. And once you have worked with someone with partial brain damage—and it may take six months or a year to get it connected—you can use that refinement on the next person who comes to you with the same need. You have developed a mechanism that you can store and replace as needed.

* * *

A teacher, as well as any other human being you share with, has to really want you to live. This is the rarest thing of all and is what stops most people from growing. Even with Nityananda, there were people who sat with him endlessly and didn't grow.

Physically, I was with him only once but I got so much because he fed me and God belched me. I feel very fortunate that way. He nourished me, but if God hadn't belched me, I would have had no chance. While Nityananda nourished me on one level, on a higher level my own spiritual connection allowed the food to be digested inside my being.

This is why you have to end your breathing exercise with your heart open and realize that you are here because I really love you. I deeply want each and every one of you to live and be free. Nothing else exists—so you are not just taking nourishment, you are given the right to digest. Until we consciously understand this, we don't take in this food and digest it. We take it in and watch it flow right out of us again. It does not stay inside our systems. Much is lost that way because of the unconsciousness that exists with the flow. You might feel a flow and you might feel a connection, but until you sigh and belch, it will not be assimilated to the degree that it would with this additional connection.

That is why I hug all of you as you come through my life. You need this contact that allows the energy to go into you with my consciousness, with my love, and with my will. You should begin to feel this with each other. If you live with somebody, feel the flow as well as the belching. Until you feel the holding and the opening that take place during that connection, you will not assimilate a fraction of the spiritual energy available to you.

CHAPTER 9

*O*ur breathing exercise has to be treated in the nature of food. As you feel the energy come and as you breathe, drink it in and digest it. You have to feel inside because unless you are aware and taking in consciously, you do not benefit. If you sat in a puddle of water unconsciously, nothing would be absorbed. But if you sat consciously, it would be absorbed into your body like a plant drinking up water. Consciousness is that within ourselves that allows us to reach and absorb in our chests. Otherwise, we are not taking in energy consciously and building our spiritual lives. Instead, we sit and assume things from our minds. Actual growth, however, is muscular—the movement of energy draws our life force through these chakras and brings it up our spinal columns. Unless we do this consciously in different ways, we will never grow and have spiritual lives. We will go off on tangents. In other words, our energy will rise to a certain point and then start to move out in that direction. That's the expression of our will.

The way to grow is to grow a little every day. To consciously absorb the energy in your system, let it roll down from your brain to your throat to your heart, through your sex organs, and up your spinal column, which refines it, to the top of your head. This kind of energy, brought in with consciousness, can change patterns. It can free you, it can enlighten you. Otherwise, you just express tensions.

To grow toward God or to grow toward consciousness is the ability of human beings to refine their energy every day and to transcend themselves. It's absolutely essential. The expression of life is to be open to people, to be open to flow, to be open to change. And compassion has to do with being free enough to surrender this one level of assumption, where we look at somebody and either feel superior or inferior. If consciously, or willfully, you take a breath and open to a flow, you can rise above any situation. Whether or not someone is superior to you, you can open and draw from that person. Or if you are looking at somebody who is not qualified in any way, you can be compassionate. This way, you always end up in a situation in which there is a life flow. And if there is a life flow, there is nourishment. You will learn and you will grow.

* * *

*T*he first thing in any kind of spiritual life is discipline. When you sit with me, keep your attention on me and on no condition look at anybody else. Never move or look at anyone else during our classes. People have their own atmospheres, and by looking at another person, you disturb that atmosphere. You make it much more difficult for them to absorb the energy around them, and any kind of communication between them and myself is ruined. So please try very hard. If it is difficult for you, close your eyes and start again. In no way do we have a right to inflict on anybody else the tensions and the curiosity that draws attention from ourselves. Try to stay open, do the breathing exercise, and bring this energy up your spine. Be as open and centered in your heart as you can be. If you are in your head, you will only get into trouble and float around in your imagination. Try to stay deeply inside and open. The sense of openness has to be there. So, between your breathing, swallow in your throat—this releases tension, it becomes energy, and it flows into the heart. By keeping your heart and the chakra below your naval open, you are free to feel the flow of energy coming down the front of you. Then be sure to wiggle around on your tailbone to release any tension and bring the energy up your spine.

When you meditate, try to feel the energy coming inside, feel the breath moving across your chest, and open your heart chakra. This is what we can relate to the most. Feel it like you feel food coming into your system when you are very hungry.

* * *

I don't know how many of you have had the experience when you eat that the food is grabbed, shredded, and digested immediately. But you should feel this spiritual energy the same way reaching inside your heart, opening deeper and deeper, asking deeper and deeper. Unless you ask to open deeper inside the heart chakra every time you work, you will not grow. Every time you work there, you must have a deeper commitment inside. And the last thirty seconds of your work, take a deep breath and ask for help to surrender negative psychic tensions. This breaks down the tensions existing between these muscles as you go from one level to another. Instead of achieving a temporary change, you destroy the internal molecularity and make any change permanent.

* * *

You have to surrender everything, even if you are attached to life itself. Take everything in you as if it were a piece of metal, throw it in the fire, and let it melt. This way, things can change and realign themselves inside. I mean, honestly, very little is going to change in a moment. It will change over a period of many moments and many years, but at least you are allowing this thing to strengthen. Like a tree that is twisted, it slowly straightens itself out and grows. You are realigning yourself, just like bad plumbing or a bad connection. You are straightening or replacing the pipes to get a better fit and a cleaner water flow. You are flushing yourself out.

We don't always know the right thing and the wrong thing. But to have this thing work in a higher sense is to let go of everything and allow a higher will—your creative flow—to have its ultimate expression.

* * *

Every human being is created with the capacity to grow and change. But the inner mechanism has to work properly. Some things that are on the tenth floor belong in the basement; other things in the basement belong on the fifth floor. By allowing this mechanism to rearrange itself naturally, we begin to recognize spirituality as an act of faith. We see by the changes that take place that it is right, that we are breathing deeper, that we feel more alive, that we can feel tensions arise and break down. It is continually growing.

I just went through something that I waited thirty years for. It finally happened. And I'm back again feeling an expansion in my brain and pain in my head. I don't question the repercussions. I certainly wouldn't say, "Is this what I've worked for?" Obviously I've worked for this because it is where I exist. And I know I can live with it much better than I could have five years or even two years ago. Inside me, the sense of being ripped from my toes to the top of my head is obvious, but my capacity to live with that condition has grown enormously. I know it will take six months for this thing to heal in me, but it will heal with much less pressure and tension and anxiety. It will heal with more gratitude from me as a person.

We have to become aware that we are paying for something. That as long as we wish to grow and breathe and expand, this thing has to feel. I mean, a seed in the ground pushes away the earth as it tries to reach daylight. Well, consciousness is something deep within us that is pushing its way up to the surface. So, we have a very simple choice—either we want it to grow, we want to learn and change, or we want to maintain what we have and feel secure. Like in a poker game, we can take our winnings and leave. Or, we can sit there and wait for the jackpot. Either way, we have to become aware of it. We have to get over this thing in ourselves that cries because this is taking place, or because we remember the things that have changed. We have to value the change that has taken place in our lives.

* * *

*A*s people, we always complain about what we don't have. However, until we have the consciousness to be grateful for what we do have, it really isn't ours. This is one of the truths in life—we have to be grateful and aware of what has changed and what good has come in our lives. By complaining and failing to enjoy those things that have changed, we do not absorb the energy or get the nourishment from our growth. And if we don't take the nourishment, we will starve regardless of the level we are on. It is as if with shelves full of canned goods, we look here and there without seeing anything, complain, and go hungry. We starve as people because we don't reach within ourselves and take that which we have already attained. We always look at the illusion of what we want, we complain about the things we supposedly are reaching for. Yet, over six months, a year, five years even, real things have come from us. We have attracted real things, things that we wanted and never believed possible. But we don't drink from them, we don't eat from them, we don't live from them. It is for only one reason—our lack of consciousness. We are ungrateful and have no value for what we have. We only express negativity for what we don't have. So, what kind of a person can't enjoy that which is there at the moment? Consciousness is having the awareness to reach out and take the nourishment to expand in your heart and express inside a gratitude for the moment.

Many people never enjoy the moment. Nothing in them can enjoy right now. They always want more and more and more, like an old lady starving to death while sleeping on a mattress stuffed with money. Many of you are like that. You are starving while you sleep on your wealth because you cannot love or enjoy or relate to what is available for you. You only complain about the things you don't have. Anyone can go into a grocery store, see what isn't there, and ask for that. Of course, you will never enjoy the meal that exists. A wise man lives on what is available and works for something else that he might want.

There are lots of things I would like—but most of them I have learned I cannot afford, and so I do without. If that person or that opportunity came, I would have to look at it and say I can't afford it at the moment. I know what I can afford and I am living it. Simplicity in what you are working for and toward must be present. Because what good is consciousness if it does not work for you?

* * *

I know that, in a sense, I gave birth to a dinosaur egg the other morning. I am grateful that it wasn't the size of a pigeon egg. When you squeeze something that size out of you, however, it breaks and pulls and tears all kinds of things. I want to raise that dinosaur and, believe me, I am not going to pay the price of giving birth to something that big and then settle for walking a couple of little spaniels down the street. That is not my idea of consciousness. I'm going to lay low for six months and nurture it until this beast can really carry me in style.

When you finally acquire whatever thing you've worked for, you have to feed it. For it to come to life, you have to nourish it. Working for a rebirth or an enlightenment is only good if afterwards you support it consciously.

If you want something or somebody or a certain situation and you get it, you have to be proud of it and you have to nourish it. You have to love it, relate to it, and keep it alive. Getting is one thing—but keeping is more important. Any fool can squeeze a situation until it becomes his, but only a conscious human being can sustain and enjoy it. Very few of you have value for the fights, the presents, and the enlightenments you receive. I'm not saying that they should make you complacent, but you should use them with awareness—and then work toward the next thing. Otherwise, you become somebody with closet skills for the dried out things of yesterday. For something to function in your life, you have to sustain the connection and the energy to nurture it. Only then can it fulfill its purpose and give you what it's supposed to give you.

Getting pregnant can be a lot of fun, being pregnant can give you some miserable times, having a child can be difficult, and raising it takes day-to-day consciousness. You have to be aware and take care of it by sleeping properly, eating properly, and being in an atmosphere conducive to the raising of this quantity, situation, or being within yourself. It's very important. I stopped living according to my nature a long time ago, and I'm very aware of it. There are times when I run into people who I knew, and seeing what their natures have done to them, I am very grateful that I've been able to choose.

For those of you who are young, longevity is the greatest of all rewards. When you run into somebody twenty years from now and see what has happened to them, you will say, "My God!" You see the ravages of misuse of the mind and the soul and the body and everything else. Because these things take their tolls so deeply, you learn through time to be grateful for the energy connections you have. And only through your conscious effort can you keep these connections open.

* * *

Did you ever go into a mediocre restaurant where they bring you your food and SLAM!—the thing hits the table. Sigh. . . . You really have to take a breath and open to start a flow between you and the food. Or, say you go into a different restaurant where the people really love the food. The waitress puts it down and her love expands your connection with the food. In everything you do, you have to feel love and a connection. You do something because you want to do it. And you want to do it because it increases the flow and connection between you and life. It is a living connection, not like a person choosing to walk down a street blindfolded.

Between teacher and student, the connection is the same. It occurs by mutual choice. You are not stuck with me. I am not your uncle or your father or your brother or your mother or someone for whom you promised to do something. You are a human being coming here out of consciousness. And if you don't come every time with a better attitude, your ability to take, assimilate, and grow becomes less. In the same way, when somebody comes into my shop as a customer or as a student, I make more of an effort. That person comes in and I see the connection between myself and life. Looking at him or her that way immediately makes a bigger flow possible. And if I do not feel particularly good that day, I say to myself, "Baby, you are not very qualified right now, so don't inflict your condition on that person."

You begin to judge yourself. You connect in spite of the way you feel. You learn to transcend your own chemistry and the tension of the day. You bring life. You do not connect down here but go to much higher levels. So, when you look at a person that you instinctively dislike—someone who reminds you of your mother or father or grandmother or an uncle who hit you—you look at the person and say to yourself, "There must be something I can relate to because I don't want to be stuck with Uncle Frank." You try to find something to relate to on a higher level. You try to feel the flow of life. If you find aspects of the person that remind you of earlier difficult situations, you put those situations aside. You do not have to tune in to them. They do not exist. And by nourishing something that is healthy, it has to come to life.

* * *

We immediately set in motion the kind of connection we have between ourselves and somebody else. I sit here and relate to every one of you to the highest part of your being. I nourish you that way and raise your level. I also raise my own level. Anybody can look at a work of art and complain about it. You can say, "Look, the feet and hands are big and the nose is this and why does it have one of these," and you can pick and pick and pick. Or you can look at it and feel the beauty and the life within it and let it carry you. A work of art should not be touched in any way by the mind. It should be a flow of energy. In the same way, when you become aware of a human being as a flowing, creative force, you relate to that instead of picking and picking and picking. Don't forget, only a crazy human being needs perfection. The closer you are to evolvement, the less perfection you need.

I mean, when people come into my store and want to spend twenty-five dollars, they really want a plastic Buddha that they can rub with a Brillo pad. It should be clean, it should be this and it should be that, and the nick on the ear or on the nose or anywhere else annoys them. They are vulnerable. The more vulnerable you are, the more perfect you need something to be. The crazier you are, the less rational you are and the more you demand from somebody else. That's why we use the word "God"—God does not demand anything from anybody. It symbolizes the level of perfection that encompasses everything. The higher the energy, the more it can complete everything. A marble torso, for instance, can sell for fifty thousand dollars. However, a connoisseur will look at its chest and back and see more than the entire statue as it once was—he will see every Greek and Roman head that ever was. He will get more than he paid for. He will see it without limitations because he knows the art.

In the same way, when you become aware of the art and creative flow in a human being, you do not need much. There is so much to love. There is so much beauty. There is so much flow. There is so much perfection. There is so much of a wonderful nature to relate to that you do not have to investigate the small things. Your bigness makes everything beautiful. The vastness of the flow within you finishes off any checks, broken pieces, or limitations. People who pick and pick and pick and pick are neurotic. They are without love.

* * *

A woman came into the store not too long ago accompanied by a child with a cleft lip and other physical deformities. It was extraordinary because the effort this woman made and the energy she put into him was unbelievable—the boy was beautiful. This little boy with his wet fingers and twisted feet looked like a piece of clay that someone, turning quickly, had dropped. And I looked at him and I looked at his mother, who walked with him proudly and talked to him like he was a brilliant human being. I looked at him and I saw a great work of art. So much had been put into him, making him beautiful and rare and extraordinary.

You have to look to yourself and ask if you could walk down the street and call this your own and live with him proudly and consciously? Very few people qualify in this sense. Go into a hospital and see what maimed and twisted and almost totally destroyed beings there are. See how hard they fight to live. And then you have to be very deeply ashamed of yourself, destroying and wasting the valuable quantity that comes to you every day. You do not value it because you have never had to fight hard enough. And yet you do not have satisfaction in your life.

So, go. There are hundreds of hospitals in the city of New York where such people live and fight tremendously for their existence. They have to fight and walk on twisted limbs and bodies and with minds that hardly function. And they fight very hard to eat and clean themselves. If you have no value for yourself, go and look after some of these people for awhile. You will understand what life is about. They have to work a thousand times harder than you with no ego involved. They suffer tremendously to function. And everything you have that you accept without gratitude, without consciousness, without ethics, is the worst reflection of spiritual energy. Watch some of these people take an hour to cross a room and then smile—they cannot afford not to smile.

You can afford not to smile, you can afford to waste your energy, you can afford to have tempers, you can afford to do a million things. You can also afford not to do your spiritual work. I cannot afford it. I cannot because I have taken on the responsibility of all of you and hundreds of others. I have to work very hard every single day because I have made a life that demands it. Until you work hard enough to build a life that forces you to work deeper, you are in danger of falling asleep and forgetting the need that exists within you.

Consciousness is growing, attracting more responsibility, and working harder. Because many of you do not have the need to work, you destroy your energy over and over again outside, making tensions and playing games that waste it. You do not work deeply enough and hard enough to have respect for it. Our work is to harness the energy, bring it inside, and refine it so that we can lift ourselves from the stupid level of games, the stupid level of ego, the stupid level of all kinds of paranoia and projection.

It has to do with using your energy—or life force—consciously in a real way, not externalizing it but internalizing it. Look at people going through the subway everyday who spend two hours traveling. They go up and down the steps slowly. You never see them pushing anybody, you never see them in any way expressing anything except their immediate conditions. They do not get caught up in externals because they cannot afford externals.

When you work deeply inside, when you harness your inner life and open inside and feel this flow and grow, you will cease being involved with external conditions, with other people, with the world situation and everything else. You will be working inside gathering your life force to serve God and transcend yourself every day. From inside yourself, you will attract more than you need to keep busy. All the outside stuff will be drawn inside because you will need it to sustain this tree of life—which is taller than a huckleberry bush. That is what growing is about. You become more and more vital and less and less spread out over the countryside doing nonessential things.

* * *

Sometimes when you work inside, you might sit, breathe, and get lost. You might go inside and disappear. So, what do you do?

You tie a string onto yourself like you would if you were going into a cave. You attach yourself to a string and consciously say, "Okay, I'm starting today. On my psychic body, on my spiritual body, I want to tie a string and watch myself." Feel yourself do it and then try to reel yourself in a couple of times an hour. Yank on the string. Make an effort and say, "Look, I really want to pull," and you pull yourself out of the maze that you let yourself get lost in. If you do this consciously while you are working, it may take six months, but it will be there—right by the front door. You will be two feet away, you will give a jerk, and the string will be there. Keep pulling until you pull yourself back into yourself.

You can't afford to sit down and allow yourself to wander off into the maze and get lost. That's not meditation. You have to constantly pull yourself back. We live by what we demand of ourselves. Finally, that demand to be here instead of out there somewhere will be inside you. Start your day by saying, "All right, here I am, I know I am going to get lost in that maze," and tie a string to yourself. The next day, tie a shorter string. And during the day, pull on it a couple of times and say, "Come on back," and you will come back. You really will. It is that simple. You have to be aware of it as a conscious effort you can make.

CHAPTER 10

*T*he only thing that has meaning in life is your connection with your spiritual work. Nothing will happen until you allow the force to work you. This energy, by its very nature, is the expression of God's will. It has nothing to do with your will, and it certainly has nothing to do with my will.

By always trying to position ourselves better, we create a membrane that separates us from the spiritual force. It is like being married to somebody and doing what you think marriage demands. You do your part—your fifty or eighty percent—except that marriage is really serving somebody else as he or she needs to be served.

It's the same in a spiritual life. You don't appease God. You don't change a little or a lot. You change as it is wanted. And the only way to find out how it is wanted is to completely surrender everything that you feel or think, good or bad. This allows a higher will to work in you. When you finally come to that point, it will change things in you. It will change the chemistry and physical manifestations. You will understand by seeing the differences in your life. *Instead of working spiritually, you will be spiritually worked.* This is what our work is about. By allowing this energy to enter you, you will wake up in the morning knowing that you were worked on in your sleep. And while this may not be what you wish for or welcome, it is something you have to surrender to. And the test of all spirituality is the ability to walk through life and not be afraid.

Everything you surrender and allow to work inside is trying to take away your thickness, the layers of callouses, the levels that we have accumulated over endless lifetimes spent on Earth. In this atmosphere, spiritual work has to do with spirit and energy. As you free yourself and the energy emerges from within, it rises and rises and rises. It rises further every time to connect with higher levels of energy. This is how your freedom takes place. You attract from your being. As you reach new dimensions, its content pours into you.

This is only possible by working—and working hard. When you take in new energy, you have to create muscles that can hold the energy and support the drama of life as you grow. This requires work. Nothing is maintained on its own, whether on the physical or spiritual level. If you don't use your muscles, they get flabby. It is a system that once maintained, you are responsible for. You increase your capacity daily by stretching the muscles and freeing energy to bring through the chakras and up your spinal column. This fuel will free you. And when you surrender, the vastness within you opens. There is no resistance because everything is there for one reason. These psychic muscles are there to open and open and open—to become a great opening through which this force works.

As it works you, you begin to understand what the flow of energy has to do with creation. It *is* creation.

When you begin to touch creation and see life come through you and bring life to other people, you understand that it is not you. Just as with parents, a child is their responsibility—not their creation. Just as a pregnant woman is a vehicle for the growth and flow of another being. On the physical level, the expression of this is our capacity to want to possess or control. It is a simple instinct. The ability to love is to free everything that you touch, not to limit it or prolong it.

In your work everyday, you have one thing to do: to open and grow and expand and feel. And I am not talking symbolically. You have to increase the column of energy that comes through you. If you don't grow every day, you will begin to have illusions of what you think you are doing. Growth has to do with breaking down resistance because every time you attain something, you have the tendency to want to think of it as yours. The only way this can take place is when the stretching becomes less. If you are not working, you are not encompassing the energy that is and was there. You are sitting back and taking credit for what happened yesterday. This is true on the physical as well as the spiritual level. You have to be conscious and work deeply to be able to transcend what was.

You no longer carry around inside this enormous bookkeeping exercise of trying to figure out how much somebody owes you and how much you give to someone else. You have no need for it because you are on a higher level. You have worked to where there is enough energy to take care of everything. It takes care of us. You have no need to take care of anything.

* * *

Something happened the other night that makes me very grateful for being able to work spiritually.

I have a tenant around the corner who is an enormous man with a very strong personality. His reasons for being are none of my business. We can't go around in life collecting information about people. There is justification for everything and it is better to stay out of people's way and let them live. Then you don't have to justify anything.

When he first moved in, I had a couple of difficult things with him. Since then, however, he's been pretty fair. But Friday, by accident, a neighbor invited me for some coffee and then I went out for the evening. When I returned later that night, the neighbor I had had coffee with earlier called to say that my tenant had left and his place sounded like a discotheque. He said there were fifty or sixty people running through the building and it was a disaster, and on and on. I said there are two options. He could forget about it or, if it bothered him, he could call the police or do whatever he felt he had to do. I said, "You're living there. I can't do anything. I'm going to sleep." He said he wouldn't call the police but would see what happened. And I went to sleep.

Even though I had had a big day in the store Saturday and I was tired, I woke up about two o'clock in the morning fighting inside myself with this tenant. It was really my unconscious working and I felt so stupid. I went back to sleep almost immediately and woke up an hour and a half later, this time really immersed in it. I sat up and surrendered deeply in myself. I understood something, not from me but from the flow of energy. And this thing said, "It is not him, it is simply a manifestation of your tension.

It needs somebody or something to jump on so it is jumping on this."

I worked with the breathing exercise for a few minutes and went back to sleep grateful to realize that it was just a thing of cause and effect on one level and, if I worked from a higher place, I could surrender it. I woke up in the morning feeling wonderful. I didn't have to run around the corner to see what had happened. Sunday night I slept fine and Monday I sent somebody up the street because the tenant called me. And he was absolutely charming. Somebody had taken his place for the weekend and he said it wouldn't happen again. There was no situation. It was like a bubble that had burst. Basically, this is how to use our work consciously. If I hadn't worked my way above the situation, the hostility in me would have kept this man from doing what he did—which was beautiful on his part. He assumed responsibility for the situation and tried to remedy it.

And this is what we do most of the time. Instead of allowing something to change, we condemn it, jump on it, and in every way abuse the situation, much like somebody spilling something on the table and instead of wiping it up carefully, getting it in the carpet and creating an even bigger mess.

Almost any situation lays on the surface until we come along and, in our attitude and the way we treat it, we make it much more than it is. We perpetuate this because we haven't learned how to use our energy in a better way. In these situations, you can stop yourself and go inside, open, and make a choice about whether you are going to lose the energy on this level or carry the situation up and drop it. If you carry anything up, you can surrender and let it fall away from you. It is the nature of anything heavy to fall from something light. You can always go down to the level of a heavy situation, embrace it, struggle with it, and enjoy it thoroughly. But if you really want to grow, then you have to not use any of your petty prejudices or anything within you that wants to categorize people. Even if you have a bad experience with somebody, if you don't allow it to change, you have to worry and eat your guts out because you don't have any other choice for your energy. You have not found a higher way to use your energy—and energy always emerges based on your ultimate use for it.

If you wish to grow, carry it up and up and up. Allow nothing to rip you off on a low level. Life has to do with how much you earn, whether it's in dollars and cents or spiritually. It has to do with what you are willing to pay for it. If you want to give more of your time and effort and if you want to grow tremendously, that's perfectly acceptable. If you don't, that's your choice and it's also acceptable. But I will not sit here and teach you.

* * *

Consciousness is spiritual energy that carries you. It is transcendent and has to do with surrender. Will deals with your capacity to say, "I want that"—and you go and get that regardless of what it costs you. Well, what it costs you may destroy a great deal of your energy. Spiritual consciousness has to do with keeping your energy inside and bringing it to a higher place to affect the change that you want in your growth. Will destroys everything in its way because it works on only one plane of existence.

On the physical level, there is will. On the spiritual level, there is consciousness. Will is visible—you know what you are working toward. Consciousness means entering an abstract area. Will is maintaining and knowing what you have. When you are working with your consciousness, you don't know.

One way to understand will is to look in the mirror and see what it costs you. Then see what consciousness costs you. Consciousness is up—it means surrender. Will is horizontal—it pushes. Love is consciousness and rape is will. Will cuts through energy levels to attain what it wants and destroys your connections. When you exercise consciousness, you connect everyone to you in a positive way and the situation rises.

When you do something willfully and it works, you say, "I did this." When you do something consciously, you say, "It happened in spite of me." It is the nature of a miracle. Tarzan standing on something and beating his chest is an expression of will. People who achieve a state of consciousness have tears of gratitude running down their cheeks. Their hearts are open.

* * *

The only way to revive yourself when you are as limp as a rag is to get starched. And the only place to do that is on a higher level. You can't get starched on the same level where you lost your energy—you have to change your chemistry.

When I'm exhausted I go where there is tremendous physical energy and I soak it up like a sponge. When I feel empty, I just sit there and, like an octopus with a thousand arms, draw in energy from the atmosphere. If you are really tired, go to Madison Square Garden when they are having an event and stand in the lobby for half an hour. Thousands of very excited people will pass you by—you are empty and they are full. So, what will happen? If you are filled with self-pity or any kind of negative quantity, the energy can't enter you. But if you are tired and open, you will get filled.

You will begin to understand that emptiness is a positive quantity that allows you to draw into yourself tremendous amounts of energy. And if you can do it when you're really ripped out, then you can do it consciously in the meditation room. When you need a more extreme situation and you are very tired, wash yourself, get dressed, and then don't go into the theatre—just stand in front of it.

I used to walk along the beach in the winter and let the wind blow through me. Just to feel a radical change in nature and my chemistry and to allow myself to be filled. If you can do it on the earthly horizontal level, eventually you can open and do it on a vertical level. You can take energy from the atmosphere and from God.

* * *

When you are in the world, stay inside yourself and try to feel the inner condition of the people around you. Use your time as an opportunity to work deeper. When I sit in the meditation room with my eyes closed, I can feel everyone there. So when you are at your job, feel the people working on your right and left. Feel the person in the back. Try to sensitize yourself and feel from the inside. Make a connection with two or three people, or even one person in the beginning. Try to feel their moods. Try to feel their needs. Communicate with them from inside so that when you talk to them you have built a con-nection. Just like weaving steel cable on a bridge, internal-ly you have to create a kind of a cable to connect you to other human beings.

Watch a mother nursing a child while she's watch-ing television or fixing dinner. She can do several things at once and so can you—and it will make life more interest-ing. It may take you a couple of years to learn to do it well. So, use your opportunities. You will find out how many times you forget and how many times you resent doing it because it means working inside. But spiritual work takes practice.

CHAPTER 11

*O*ur work is based on being able to absorb the atmosphere in which we live and, basically, a strong life makes for very strong energy and very strong tensions. When we don't fight the situation that brings about the tensions but accept it consciously and in a state of surrender, the energy is absorbed deeply within us. Tension, pain, all of these things are heavy energies and because they are—instead of just going into us, they go very deeply into us.

In some desert areas, they put grass seed in little pellets of earth or clay that when thrown out of an airplane dig deeply into the earth and grow and hold the soil. In the same way, when we surrender deeply and open and absorb tensions and pain, we really are digging into our unconscious. We are using our energy to dig into this unconsciousness and free the material and spiritual wealth that is an internal condition and available for us. But it is against the nature of people because we always try to live without feeling any kind of pain. It is our ignorance, our simplicity, our stupidity, our true lack of development that always allows us to attract situations that become difficult.

We all have the experience of meeting somebody, getting involved, going through six months or a year, and finally understanding where we were wrong. Then we see the person differently. Not that we see so differently, but we see that the person represented something we needed. We needed the connections to take that particular energy. Once we've used that energy and grown above the situation, we haven't the capacity to bring the other person and the situation to a higher level. So we begin to see them as they are or were from the beginning. We should always consciously raise our personal situations to higher levels so that they can serve us again and again.

* * *

*I*t is the nature of people to find ways to reject something. Why? Because average human beings lack the capacity to reinvest in another human being. We always look and feel disappointed, we feel rejected, we feel a million things that represent putting energy into something that doesn't exist. And why analyze something that doesn't exist? We say, "This person is incapable of doing this" or "They're always ripping me off" or other negative expressions of, in a sense, the hole in the person. Yet we continually pour our energy into these voids instead of trying to bring about another connection that will raise the person and make a vital human being.

Because of my own nature, I am trying very hard to change the level of my being, the level of my spiritual work, and the level of my life. And I mean exactly that—not one level, but many levels simultaneously. The nature of creation is that we have multiple levels or multiple dimensions of capacity. When one is not functioning for some reason, we can consciously use our creative energy to develop another talent or function. This means that our mechanism can work completely and that our life energy is used consciously twenty-four hours a day. Most of the time we focus on what is not functioning instead of seeing how we can consciously use our energy at a particular moment in an area that is functioning within us. We are so busy questioning our lack of capacity in two or three other places that we don't take the alternative possible for us and use the capacity that we have.

Only a fool continually finds rejection. An intelligent human being looks for the alternative. When 1, 2, and 3 are closed, use 4. If 4, 3, and 2 are closed, then 1 is available. Sometimes you can have half of 1 working and half of 3 working. An infinite combination of capacities, alternatives, and dimensions always exists. And we only find them when we discover that when something we look toward doesn't function, instead of whining about it, we switch to something we can do. This is common sense.

* * *

Where we fail enormously is in thinking that we have common sense. Common sense is the rational thing to do. Unfortunately, we always overpraise our condition. People are not rational, people are not normal, and certainly people do not have the capacity to detach from one thing and go to another. When we stop trying to give ourselves the values we set up for ordinary human beings, we come closer to the truth of our situation. This madness, this incapacity to function freely, really expresses the human race more than anything else. Once we understand that, we begin to see the need that exists within us to consciously make efforts that we will not make rationally.

A rational effort requires a free human being. And until you are free, until you have this freedom within your sense of being, until you have the ability to go to the right or left or frontward or backward or up or down, you do not qualify for the label of a free human being. Stop thinking of yourself as being a rational person. Stop thinking of yourself as someone who has control. After a lifetime of very intense work, I see that when a lot of money comes around, my incentive drops dead. I watch these things in me that are completely at the whim of need. I work under pressure—we all work under pressure—and I have to sit down and consciously talk to myself to get moving because there is no outer pressure motivating me. And I am grateful that I don't have this insane drive that some people have to pile up vast amounts of money. I really have to work consciously.

I find that I have to identify emotionally in a conscious way so that I don't just go this way and that way. I really am grateful because twenty years ago I was like a reed blown on the wind—any way the wind blew, I went. I remember this very distinctly. One of my great wishes, one of the things I endlessly asked for inside was to be delivered from this possession of emotion and energy beyond my control. And I haven't forgotten these things. I try to stay detached because of the effort it has taken me to get this far.

Within ourselves we have to understand our madness, our imbalance, our lack of control. It's a terrible thing and so many people suffer abysmally because they think everyone else is in control while they are not. They feel cursed that they must work harder and deeper while it comes easier for somebody else. That's crazy. Everybody in this world is working toward some kind of balance. There is always something swamping them and a million things to consciously work at. Unfortunately, people are not honest enough to speak up and express their situations.

* * *

There is never a time during spiritual development when you are breaking through one level and going to another that you don't live like a madman. This condition is always there because a very strong and violent energy is breaking out of the "you" locked inside yourself. Through more energy, you are free to see this is your state. And these passive people who could kill everyone, well, these things truly exist. Somebody who has an enormous need to be successful, to be in control, to be a teacher—all of these thousands and thousands and thousands of things exist in various assortments in all human beings. Underneath a great timidity lies a tremendous violence. Maybe not a violence toward people in general but maybe toward parents.

These things exist within people and unfortunately it is not recognizable because we can't afford to allow ourselves to see our true condition. If we can become honest, understand it, face it, and realize that we are working to get control over and transcend these things, we can be open. We can be grateful to the people we love who we are using at this particular moment to feed us and give us the security to transcend these different parts of ourselves. We have a chance for realization on a very, very, very high level. Otherwise, we will have a realization, but it will be the realization of a moron.

And there are people who do that. They become crystallized and in their crystallization they freeze everything that is a limitation. They never burn or utilize this locked-in energy to grow further. And growth should be infinite. We can refine and refine and refine until we look at ourselves and realize that three years ago we had the sensitivity of a goat in heat—and now we can function like a well-trained dog.

* * *

Slowly but surely we find ourselves growing and growing and growing. The need to think of ourselves as being pure, however, is outrageous ego. If we had any idea of the thickness of a human being's molecular density against this infinite energy that flows through the atmosphere that we call the *atman* or spiritual force, it would frighten us to a point that we would find it impossible to work. But we live in a state of grace. God is an extraordinarily generous and good energy so that we live in an atmosphere that is barely possible for us to sustain and that allows us to move to the next level. We are structured in a way that we always have the ability to rise to another level and then to another and another. It is an infinite amount of work. And only because of infinite grace is life structured in a way that allows us to get here and then visualize this and think of that and go on and on and on. The endlessness, the ability to live this way finally allows us to expand and love everything and everybody, to include the entire universe within ourselves.

I certainly don't claim to be enlightened. I certainly don't claim anything other than that I am a million times further than I was a few years ago. I know when I sit down and look at you my heart breaks and opens because I really love you. This tremendous feeling rises in me and I look from one to the other and so much of me responds only in a positive way. I really understand your need. I really understand how some of you can't open, that you can't afford to do more than you're doing in this particular moment. I try to kick you a little bit and I try to love you a lot, to give you the nourishment to open more. Some of you don't have the guts, some of you don't have a pattern structurally that allows for more than what is there in a particular moment.

This is your acceptable limitation because if you really work and do the breathing exercise as it is given, if you really feel the energy and the nourishment in your organs, these organs will grow strong. It's just a question of feeding muscles. Spiritual work is nothing more than millions of muscles taking in nourishment and growing and as they grow they manifest. Everything in life manifests. Everything shows the level of its existence. As we reach a richer level of spirituality, it shows images and paintings that are extraordinary. Slowly but surely you rise above that into a richer color and energy sense, less a manifestation of figures and more a manifestation of color. That goes on until it becomes a more and more rarified atmosphere and slowly you become free. This struggle within you is really only you eating energy, feeding muscles, and feeling the tensions and pain that these muscles go through as they open. It is simple.

* * *

We have a very simple yoga practice. That energy manifests is the problem—because we can imagine a lot, we can visualize a lot, we can sense a lot. The less we sense, the less mind we use. The fewer emotions we use, however, the more capable we become of taking in energy and allowing ourselves to accept our growth simply. The tensions we make and the limitations we put upon ourselves really are the problem—there really is no limitation. Finally, as we grow more, we can take in the pain as these muscles and bones expand inside. The pain only represents growth. We can drink it in and have our hearts open simultaneously. That we can take in this pain with gratitude means we have a chance to make a great leap, a leap that will allow us to burn faster, take in faster, and give off more.

It must be understood that what you can't surrender must be accepted as your limitation. It is only your stubbornness and resistance. You have to talk and fight yourself because you are letting something gain control. You are lazy or stupid and it is as simple as that. There is no excuse for ignorance. There is no excuse for anything because doing, working, just taking a breath enables you to eat through the tensions that keep you from making this effort. It is so simple. Do this for half an hour once or twice a day and try in your ordinary relationships with people to internalize the situation. Do not identify and talk and talk, but drink in and feel the flow of life between you and another human being. Be grateful that you are using your energy in a positive and simple way.

* * *

When you start to feel like stone, when you feel that thickness, it means you are working through a shell that you have always lived on the outside of. This allows the nourishment within you to rise and expand—and the shell has to break away. Be grateful that you feel the shell. Most people live above that in a world of illusion. This shell is very real.

In the same way, some of you will do our meditation practice for a few months and feel a band around your head. It is like a one-inch band of steel that shows you are scratching the surface below whatever it is that you wear in the world for protection. People walk around saying, "Oh, I love everybody and everything, blah, blah, blah." But if you look behind them, there's total disaster. They destroy everything they go near. They give bad advice to everyone they touch. Everything they do is terrible. Work for six months and you will finally melt away this external mass and begin to understand that you are an uptight person. You will feel this band around here that usually takes six months to a year to break—it is a real band of tension that we live with.

We can't afford to realize what our condition actually is—it's so bad. Only after working in a positive way do we begin to see that we have a lock on our heart and a band of tension around our head and a bar of steel on our shoulders. These things go away as we come out of this prison that we have built. What you are feeling is very real and you should be grateful for it. Your brain will loosen up and you will begin to breathe differently. One of the first things that takes place after that is that your skin will change. So feel it, but don't think about it. When you think about it, you feed it. When you surrender it, you dissolve it. This band of tension is a gift, it is an achievement, and you say, "Thank God I've come to that level." As it dissolves, you will slowly absorb the tension and one day it will be gone.

* * *

*A*re we wrapped in this life to look like a Christmas package? It's like putting twenty or thirty years of garbage in a lead container where you can't smell it. You paint it with stars and sprinkle it with gold dust and put a couple of cherries over here and say, "What a great Christmas present." God help you when you break it open. It begins to break open and we see this thing and think, "This is the reward for working?" Of course it's the reward for working! Would you prefer this stuff to eat into your kidneys and eat into your heart and eat into your mind and eat into every organ in your body? It has to stink as you begin to clean up this mess that you call "you."

But we don't want to pay. We always get to a point, we improve a little bit, and then somebody loves us because they see we have grown spiritually. So this thing goes "clunk" and closes and you're walking and holding hands with someone who's been closed for twenty-three years and you've been closed for twenty-five years. A perfect marriage. And then what do you do? You give birth to some poor thing that comes through you and your trash heap, this accumulated cosmic mulch pile, and then you are really breeding through this terrible thing that has existed in you forever. This is what we're cursed with.

I couldn't understand this in myself and so when I was with the Shankaracharya of Puri, I said, "I want to grow and I want to suffer."

He said, "That's not right. You should say you want to grow and you want to be happy."

So I finally said, "Yes, I want to grow and I want to be happy."

And he said, "You're going to suffer like a jackass for twenty-five more years," and I started to laugh. I said, "Well, why?"

He said, "Because of the way you were conceived. You were conceived in tremendous hatred. Your mother and father hated each other violently, and your soul was locked in this tension."

And I really began to understand. It's not their fault. It's nobody's fault. This is your karma and your ball game. You either play the game, break through it, and clean it up—or you don't. It's not going to change. Hating them is going to perpetuate it, just like the bands on your head. If you are thinking about it, you keep making that kind of poison. Accept it. Surrender it. Be grateful that you can at least know what is wrong. I mean, until you have a diagnosis, until you have consciousness, you can't take care of it. The ignorance of our situation makes us the prisoner. Our ability to grow inside breaks and takes away these bonds and really frees us. Nobody did it to you—it was. Whatever it was, they spun the wheel, the number "6002XYZ" popped up, and out you came. You got this kind of a selection.

Within you, however, is also the ability to cope with it. The tensions and problems you were born through are chemical components that, when ground down, make the particular fertilizer that nourishes the kind of a plant you are.

This is the perfection of this life. When you take all of the quantities, both negative and positive, when you grind them down, put one teaspoon in a glass of water, and drink it, you are a free human being. All this stuff you call your karma is exactly what you need to become free. But we live our karma, we never dissolve it, and so we don't become free. That's the rubbish we get loaded on when we talk about spirituality and the "Path."

The Path is learning to accept all of the garbage and an authentic spiritual practice dissolves it and grinds it down completely. This frees you to finally become a human being. Why live with this limitation? It's ridiculous. It's acceptable because we really want to go through the drama. We hate ourselves to the degree that we are willing to spend our whole lives fighting this or fighting that. It's crazy. Karma is a human being's accepted imprisonment. It's how much garbage life can drop on you that you find bearable and are willing to survive with. It makes no sense at all. Consciousness is finishing up that karma in as short a time as possible and being a free human being—not to have it as your guideline, but to have it as something to take care of as soon as possible. As a free person you will be able to choose spiritually what you want. All the things we think about, all the things we react to are really karmic situations and karmic limitations.

CHAPTER 12

*T*he miracle of our existence is that we as people sit together in abysmal ignorance of our potential. Nothing in us can really understand how deep creativity is and how infinite is every human being's capacity to grow. Until we pass through the doorway of one dimension into another, we have no sense of a rebirth or any difference. And so, on one level, we play like some animals in a mudhole, throwing little things at each other.

The purpose of growing is to take the nourishment, to reach from where you are into a totally different universe with different energies, different rules, and certainly a different consciousness. Growing is only that. It is only taking in nourishment and developing the ability to receive and feel inside a connection like that between a mother and child. It is an umbilical cord that draws. It is a mutual drawing that illustrates how my growth feeds you and takes back what is being replaced. You can't fill something unless you empty it. This lets you put into it and take out and put into it again and again. It is impossible, therefore, to study intellectually or in any way will the mind to learn. This only creates congestion. It only thickens the content and puts it under more pressure. Growing is an emptying out and a filling up that allows you to begin refining and purifying and nourishing. Through this nourishment, the muscles in the body, in the chakras, in every tissue and organ, begin to sprout and grow.

As you grow, it is essential to rid yourself of the congestion that results from the refinement of your energy. Every day you should consciously take a deep breath in your heart and surrender negative psychic tensions and congestion. If you don't flush it out, it will reform again. You can't change a pattern in your life or free yourself unless you rid yourself of the unassimilated and lower forms of energies. And so you slowly rise. Every time you work you continually break up your energy, separating it just like you would churned milk—the butter you keep and the lesser product you throw away. The lesser product is really what we use—or should use—to live with in our ordinary day and in our relationships. This is the by-product of life.

The real product of life is the ability to take our creative force and continually raise it to a higher level. In this way, we live organically and naturally. The change that occurs doesn't take place from our minds, it takes place strictly from this churning of creative energy as we endlessly bring it around and around and around.

This is what is unique in India when we see someone who has tremendous spirituality. It is not the person's wisdom but rather God's wisdom that detaches from them and creates this conscious state of being. Such a person when asked might give an incorrect answer. However, from this force that doesn't have a voice as we understand it, a voice speaks. It doesn't have a mind as we understand the mind, but it communicates from itself. We don't have to talk. We simply have to surrender and allow the consciousness of this higher energy to function.

When you went to someone like Nityananda, if you were open, you heard. It spoke in you. It advised you. It nourished you. It fed you and in every way was the teacher. It wasn't the man. It wasn't the voice of the man. It wasn't the intelligence of the man. It was a state of being that came from the conscious use of his energy, separating and creating another dimension and another level of life.

Only when we get involved in this need to think, to rationalize, to emotionalize do we begin to understand the limitation of a person and the remarkable quality of a state of being. It *is*. We continually try to understand something that is in the mind, or in our emotions, or within our physical body. But it is this detached energy, this state of being, that is remarkable. This, in fact, is the first stepping stone into the cosmos because it allows us to remove ourselves from everything of the earth and take in this nourishment. From this, we can begin to attract on every higher level.

* * *

There is nothing rational about spiritual work because spiritual work does not exist in its true form on the earth. As a lighter and more refined energy, it has a different density and exists in a completely different dimension. The only way to understand it is from the results in our lives, by the feeling of a connection that nourishes and feeds us. We are not working correctly when we succumb to all the tensions in the mind, to all of the talking, to all of the things inside that are trying to mutilate the energy. Leave it alone. Really work to drink it in and rise above yourself. This is the advantage of a state of being or a state of spiritual energy that is moving. We either rise with it or we get underneath it where the tensions of this physical life exist. And growing is exactly that.

I was very fortunate when I was younger to be given the opportunity to live with a great saint. But I couldn't step into a room in his presence. I had to push my feet. I would lay on the floor, put my foot against the doorjamb, and push myself into the room. There was such an energy for me as well as a double resistance in me to go in. Like being in a wine press, I felt myself being squeezed out and this force going in. I put myself under that kind of pressure. I wished for it and lived with it for some thirty years. When you are new to this work and fight this pressure, you are fighting with yourself to not allow this energy in, to not allow it to be assimilated so that it can really render from your being, you. You are the conflict. You are against your own growth. It is your ego fighting for its existence and it comes up with a million stupid reasons. It's the thing that allows you to attract a theater date on the night that you should come to a meditation class. Or it allows you to express your energy fighting with somebody instead of opening, absorbing that energy, and rising above the situation.

There is nothing rational about fighting because fighting and tensions only destroy creative energy. The ability and desire to fight is only the unconsciousness in a human being that will not draw in the energy and rise above it. The same energy that is wasted externally, if drawn in and internalized, will allow us to rise above the situation and see that it is ridiculous. It's crazy to use our energy in any way except as nourishment and growth.

* * *

I lived with many saints in different parts of the world. I sat with them for weeks and months doubting myself. And I'd look at them and ask myself, "Who asked a question today? Who wanted? Nobody." Nobody. And you can sit all over the world in temples in Japan or in India or in China or anywhere and listen to the stupidity that goes on daily. Nobody comes with a wish inside. Nobody has their heart tearing apart because of their desire to find the growth that is available. Only through that do you qualify. Only through that do you express your wish. I mean, I am going to be forty-five years old in two weeks and I'm still burning inside. I still have this wish, this thirst inside to grow, and it drives me crazy. And I can qualify, I can stand next to anyone, but who wants to be measured against anyone else? The only one to be measured by is God and the only thing to work toward is to get there. Competition on a low level of existence has no meaning.

* * *

*I*t breaks my heart when I see people not wanting to grow. Every day for me is a burning that, in my heart and soul, I never wish to inflict on anyone else. To serve you, I have to completely destroy within myself today everything that existed for me yesterday. In this way I don't crystallize. I don't want to become secure enough to think that I've gone far enough to qualify for what somebody else calls enlightenment. I don't want that. I want to die open and I want to go up. All of the intelligence, crystallization, and intellectualism can stay here and be eaten by those people who want to eat yesterday's truth. It's only a dead truth.

Truth means continually destroying within yourself everything that existed a moment before. If you have a need to hold onto anything, then you will not have realization and you will not have within a sense of serving others. You will be a person who offers death to other people because you haven't the capacity to go through the cycle of rebirth and death in yourself. Either you want to grow to such depth that you always feel inside the cycle of death and rebirth, or you don't qualify to do this work. I would rather have students leave early on than sit here and become a limitation for myself or anyone else. Undoubtedly we have the most difficult spiritual work available. You have to make up your mind whether you really wish to grow and surrender "you" or hold on to a million extraneous things that haven't nourished anybody for two, four, six, eight, or ten thousand years. We don't need the past, we need the moment.

We have the capacity inside to assimilate the energy as it comes into the universe. It has to go inside us and root out everything that existed, not only in this life but in every past life. The only thing I promise you is an extraordinary life. You will see in yourself and in your connection with others a living and creative experience. You will see and understand, and it will break your heart a thousand times to see how deeply people say they are looking and how remarkable they are in their creative capacity to avoid finding. The most creative capacity in human beings lies in their unconscious effort to not find what they say they're looking for. It is unbelievable how people can make a string of coincidences a million miles long to get them out of doing what they could do simply by crossing the street. It is this, really, that continually destroys people who say they're growing and wish to grow. They stop growing because they lack the energy to sustain their search and their evolvement.

It is our dedication to reach toward this endlessness that has to do with creative capacity. We are like any other organic thing that lives. We have to live each day as it comes and not live in the past. We have to open and allow this energy inside to burn up whatever was there. From this compost heap of life, we see smoke rising as we take in this energy and loosen up deeply within ourselves the unconsciousness that is so strongly embedded there. In this way, we free ourselves and find that we can breathe. We find that our chakras are not limited to our physical body but reach out into infinity. From thousands and thousands of years and millions and millions of miles we can draw the energy we need.

* * *

Spirituality and cosmic consciousness should not be so many words. They should be a living reality that we can come to within ourselves every single day and see our world expand and feel every muscle within us open and become the nourishment that frees us. It frees our hearts, it frees our eyes, it frees our minds, it frees every chakra within us so that we are not slaves of these organs. Instead we are free to feed them and have them expand and flow one to the other and bring us the nourishment that allows us to get above the earth.

* * *

You have the right to be free in this life but you have to really want it. If you ever have a question, ask it. If you are unable to follow the breathing exercise, sit every night until you understand. It is not wrong to not be bright, it is not wrong to not be clever. It is only wrong to stay stupid, to not question again and again. You have to think, you have to feel inside, you have to question, you have to really want inside very deeply. This will make a vitality that will feed all of us. To sit complacently, however, to not wish, to not want, to not burn inside—these are limitations. The only thing that doesn't burn is a wet mattress or wet newspapers. To be free, you have to open and bring this wish inside.

It is heartbreaking to see the lack of depth in so many of you. You don't ask and open and ask and want. I personally have so much energy. I have as much to give you as a fleet of trucks backing up to the Hudson River and pouring in millions of gallons of milk. Instead, my energy goes out into the atmosphere because there isn't among all of you enough people to want what I have. And so I work and grow because I keep going around and around and around in myself. But I do need communication. I really want people who want to ask, who want to take, and who want to grow. And it is your wish that qualifies you—it is your heart and your mind wanting so much. Some of you are ten lifetimes ahead of others, but being superior doesn't mean anything. In six months of working you can be ahead of somebody who might have been five hundred lifetimes ahead of you. It is the nature of the energy in the universe at this moment. It has such richness and such capacity to feed and nourish you that there need be no limitation. There need be no time lag because you grow from your ability to take in at this moment. Last year or ten years ago has nothing to do with the moment. We are living in an expanded consciousness, which means that the energy in the atmosphere today is richer than it was a day ago or a week ago or a month ago.

It is easy to break up inside all of your patterns and all of your limitations. There is no reason not to work and not to grow. Sit here and drink it in. Feel your muscles devour this energy, feel yourself grow inside and open. And if you can't make yourself hungry, if you can't express that, then sit at night and ask and ask and ask. You have to ask endlessly. You can ask for four hours or fifty thousand times until you find within you such a wish to grow and such an openness that your hunger allows you to take in a thousand times more. There is no limitation to a person's capacity to take in and grow. The only thing is that once you've taken ten times, you have to do it for the rest of your life. For it to stay within you, you have to sustain an increase. In other words, if you work twice as much tonight, then you will have to work twice as much plus one tomorrow. There is no such thing as a spiritual cram course. Anything attained must be sustained by the same amount of work that went into the attainment. Therefore, to have a real result, you have to increase your work every single day. You can't work twice as much on Fridays because you want to stay out weekends. There is no such thing. Spiritual work is a conscious flow of energy through the chakras every single day. And it takes at least half an hour's effort to get the chemistry flowing that will allow this thing to grow in you.

* * *

*I*f you want to grow, then sit and ask inside and really bring your mind inside. It's the same as if you had a child who was dying. You would pray and ask God and find that the emotion opened your heart. You would ask, even if you claimed not to believe in such a thing. Do you understand?

You have to ask inside. And you keep asking inside and hear yourself say, "I want to grow." You keep repeating that until you hear the superficiality of it and then you hear the emotionality of it and then you feel your heart really break open because you've asked so much that you're bringing energy into the heart chakra. You keep asking and asking and asking and the nourishment inside suddenly expands and your heart opens. Then you have a place to grow from. You have really opened your heart to your wish, not from your mind, but from your heart. So you take it from your heart and you bring your mind there and you say inside, "I want to grow." You keep saying this out loud until you hear the tone change in your voice, until you feel the emotion change in your voice, and then you keep saying it until you feel your heart break open.

* * *

*T*he reason we don't progress is not through a lack of deep breathing. It is because we don't take the breath down far enough and hold it long enough. This is where we fail. We work and satisfy ourselves without satisfying the chemistry within us. If we take a little longer in our breathing and wait a little longer in our opening, we free a different kind of chemistry. There's a depth in us that has this chemistry, and by taking a little longer, more of it emerges. Our lack of chemistry is exactly what this burning is about. It is what the asking is about. We do it but we don't do it deeply enough. We don't do it long enough. We very rarely do things that have that capacity. When we love somebody, we wait for one minute. We feel a little flow and then we look over here or we look over there. But if this thing takes so long to get moving, it makes sense to hold onto it longer and feel it more.

* * *

*S*tudent: I feel myself open up when I'm with you—which surprises me every time. Why can't I stay open with the other people in my life?

Rudi: Well, how can you? You're talking from your mind and it's coming out your mouth. You finally have something open in your heart. You should bring the energy down from your mind to your heart to the base of your spine and up again. Instead you're so happy that it's going to your heart that you bring it from your heart to your mouth and out. This does you no good at all. And this is what everyone does when the energy finally starts to flow. You are like a beggar who is so grateful to get a quarter that you don't have your hat out for the next person who was going to give you ten thousand dollars. You begin to have an experience and you say, "Oh my God, it's happened." Then it's gone.

Breathe the energy down, bring it inside, bring it to your sex organs, bring it up your spine, hold onto your gratitude for half an hour. Let it flow around and around and around, saturating your body and feeding every muscle. Then you will be open for your wife, you will be open for your children, you will be open for me, you will be open for everyone else. You limit your own experience. Having an experience means you have finally worked something to a point where it begins to change its chemistry. But you have to take it from first base to second base to third base and then home. Why limit it at that point? We never work deeper, we never work long enough, we never carry it where it can do us good.

You think that it is in your heart, but six months from now when a shark comes along, your heart closes and all of it is wasted. You have to start over. It's like mining—every time you want a handful of gold or silver, you have to dig from here to the corner. If you build a structure, however, you can go inside anytime and take out whatever you want. Any experience is only as good as your conscious ability to do it at will. Take the energy, bring it deeply inside, and let it nourish your whole system. Don't become a victim of your own limitation.

Usually what we do is react to situations. We react to our bodies, we react to our minds, we react to our emotions telling us what to do. If it says "go there," then you go over there. Only a fool follows his mind. Only a fool follows his emotions. If you go the other way, you become free. You should only go toward nourishment and growth.

Anything else is a limitation. By staying centered and working above it, you can encompass your limitations and grow.

CHAPTER 13

*A*s our work progresses, there has to be an increasingly deeper capacity both in myself as a teacher and in you as students. As a teacher, I have to support a commitment for the first time with people who I feel will be with me for the rest of my life. It is very different because when we sit down and say, "Fine, I'm going to do this" or "I'm going to do that," something inside us opens. First one layer opens, and possibly a second layer, and then even a third layer. We have within us an endless number of structures—hundreds or thousands, it doesn't matter how many. But we also have a lack of capacity because of past experience not only in past lives but in this life because we have never found a depth that satisfies us. So we expose ourselves just enough so that when the situation shifts, we aren't really hurt. We also lack the capacity to fight and keep the change from taking place in a way that separates us. If we were more flexible, we would hold on and this thing would eventually become a higher level of that relationship.

Finally, it became obvious to me that some students were really fighting to have a deeper connection with me. I found that I had to understand that and open inside to a much deeper connection with them and with all of you. It is difficult for us to accept the superficiality of our lives and the superficiality of our dedication. Only when somebody calls for more do we open more. It was this call to me by some of you that allowed me to see my own self-protectiveness. Ultimately, it is the difference between creating tensions or having a real flow of energy between us. Tensions grind away the energy that we are taking. We think and we emotionalize and we grind away this flow that is trying to come in and feed us.

Our work is really a straight-line feeding that gives you the energy and nourishment you need to open and allow the roots of your own creativity to spread out and reach into the atmosphere. In this way, you find your own connection with God. I am not possessive—not that I don't love some of you tremendously. But being possessive would make it impossible for me to offer you the freedom that I want for myself. Not that I didn't once have a possessive nature, but it was torn out of me. I honestly don't have it now and I am very grateful to offer you everything I have in return for your wish to grow.

Understand that everything you do in your mind and emotions destroys the energy that is given to you. It is your ego, this thing that cannot allow itself to be exposed and see its stupidity and limitation. Only when you have the ability to listen to your own call for life, only when you deeply want from your own heart to serve God and to serve your own growth will this process take place in you. It is a conscious process. You have to feel yourself consciously reaching and taking the energy from the atmosphere. You have to feel it flowing through you.

* * *

When some people say they are perfect, it doesn't mean they are. It means they have an ego that allows them to claim perfection. But there is no such thing because either they are changing and growing or they are totally limited and can only limit you. I am growing and I can see my limitation, I can see my stupidity, I can see the need to grow in myself—and this allows you to grow. If I am closed, as students you will never have a chance to be free. Regardless of where you go in life, you must understand that people who claim perfection are crazy. They are limited, regardless of how big they might seem to be. They have taken their development and put a top on it. After a while, it becomes paranoia—because any restriction to creative energy becomes an encompassed force that, as it is attacked, has to protect itself. It builds a wall that becomes thicker and thicker and thicker.

* * *

We are living in a time of expanding energy. The nature of our growth is that everything that comes into us and everything we become attached to has to expand. Everything it feeds becomes mature and that maturity expresses itself in detachment. We become freed from something. We become, in a sense, secure inside so that we can come and go freely. And the reason we don't have fifty thousand people in our practice is because I haven't poured into this energy a glue to bind people. If I needed to do that, I would limit myself as well. You can't limit somebody and not find yourself in turn limited. You must have a very deep wish to grow. You must open inside and express your life in terms of energy and nourishment.

You will feel a positive growth that frees you from the illusion and the attachment of your life. You will feel an increased hunger and a need for more nourishment. Your love and your sense of growth give you the capacity to work deeper, to take in more, and to see around you a growing positive quality and quantity. That you feel the love and respect expressed idealistically in advanced spirituality as paradise doesn't become your limitation. You begin to understand that there is no end and no limitation. You only reach a paradise where you collect the energy to go off into this abstract universe. And the further you go in growing, the further you go away from the earth. As if you took off in a rocket ship, you finally see this thing diminish and disappear. And you are in space—deep inner space. This is infinity.

* * *

It takes a long time to have the fuel and the courage inside to detach from the things that we call our universe. Human beings finally must have, within their own minds and hearts, the ability to expand to these infinite places from growth—not from ego. It is a very simple thing. Each day, you take some of your life energy, draw it inside, and let it rise to the top of your head. As it keeps cycling around refining itself, you acquire the capacity to store some of your life force. You become like any other healthy plant. You become something that has in its root system the ability to sustain a storm, the ability even to be frostbitten and come back to life.

You have the ability to accumulate this life force. And it is your capacity to store life and retain it in your body that allows you to be above any situation. You can see with your own eyes and understand in the seeing. It's incredible. Sometimes I show somebody an art object or a painting and they don't see it because they are so caught up in the drama. This is an expression of where they are and where they haven't developed.

Understand that the only way to grow is to begin accumulating the energy internally to nourish all of your organs and sensitivities. Only then will they mature and enable you to not be shocked by your own limitations.

* * *

This weekend a student asked about her heart and her inability to feel. I looked at her and I saw a flush toilet and the little water tank with the lever you pull. I looked at her and realized that this girl wastes so much emotion that when she comes to the point of trying to flush herself or draw in the energy, she is like somebody who walks into the bathroom right after someone else has left, does her thing, and then pulls the lever. Nothing happens because there is no water pressure. She waits two minutes when it takes the tank eight minutes to fill up again. She keeps pulling the lever and pulling the lever and pulling the lever and pulling the lever—it has no effect.

It has no effect because you have to wait long enough. You have to feel energy accumulate in your heart. You have to feel your breathing and your ability to open up and feel your heart. Just like a flushed toilet you feel it slowly filling up. Then you take your second breath and bring the energy down through the chakras, through the sex organs, and up your spinal column. It is better to wait and take ten times longer. For it to be effective, you have to experience this. You can't be so anxious for an effect—let your internal mechanism tell you. You can feel in your heart whether this thing is full enough to take another breath and bring the energy down. If it's not, it means that you are working and not getting a result.

This is true of any effort you make if you are sitting and not working in a real way. If you have a lot of tension or feel tight in the head, or if you fantasize a lot, then just as in a laundromat, do a pre-soak. Take a small breath in your nose and let it enter your brain. Feel this breath accumulate in your mind and in your emotions, and begin to relax. Feel it start to warm the air, the breathing, and your concentration. Still feeling the energy, relax and swallow in your throat. Because some of your breath is releasing tensions and bringing down more energy, you can begin with a heavier force of conscious energy.

* * *

When you are emotional, you cannot speak from a spiritual place. Because you are not centered inside, you talk like a jackass. If you can't speak with any depth, if you can't understand, how do you expect to hear what I'm saying to you. You are talking exactly as you would if you met somebody in the street and started to discuss the seven o'clock news. You are having a discussion. You are not asking a spiritual question from a place inside that can receive and give you more consciousness. I could talk to you for fifty years like this but it will have no impact because you don't go to the right place in yourself. I hear the voice you use in Bloomingdale's or at the grocery store. You are talking from exactly the same place. How can you possibly expect to get a result unless you go inside?

If you have a problem doing anything, go into your heart and ask and ask and ask. If you don't ask from your heart, you are not asking from a place of depth. You can reduce the breathing exercise to the simplest thing in the world and at least ask me a question by taking a breath inside and speaking from your heart. After all, if I was busy thinking about my business and you came and asked me something, how could I possibly communicate with you? You would sense it and be insulted that your effort wasn't valued.

Have as much value for your spiritual work as you have for other things. Open your heart and say, "I want to feel an expansion in my heart. I want to ask a question from here." If people came all day asking me questions without depth behind them, not only would there be no growth, I would choke to death. Again, you must surrender and ask. If you are stuck in your brain, remember—I can hear you.

* * *

Go inside your heart and spend six hours if you have to. Take a breath in your heart and ask inside, "I wish to surrender." Keep talking until you hear where you are speaking from—until you realize that you are shallow. Then breathe into your heart, keep asking inside, and drill a hole in your heart. Keep asking and asking and asking. I mean, if somebody came into your house in the middle of the night, put your finger on a chopping block, and said he was going to cut it off, you would dig inside yourself and probably plead for it, right? You would plead for the finger. Well, certainly your finger is nothing compared to the heart inside you that is not functioning correctly. We'll fight for a finger, we'll fight for an ear, we'll beg somebody to spare the life of somebody else—but we won't go inside or realize that this thing is dead.

Your heart might as well be made of glass or marble. It doesn't function. And it's more than a finger. If you pleaded from your heart with this person for your finger, you would be shocked if he didn't respond. And yet, when it is the heart inside you that doesn't open when you ask, it is a terrible thing. You can watch television and hear how a five-year-old child's kidneys are failing. You will sit there in front of the TV crying that this is a tragedy. But that is not a tragedy for you—that your own heart doesn't function is a tragedy for you.

* * *

*H*ere is an exercise. Let your right hand hang down at your side and don't look at it. First, feel your pinky and then sense the next finger and the next and next and finally the thumb. Begin to feel the palm of your hand and your wrist on the inside and outside. Feel it begin to pulsate with life and then begin to feel the back of your hand. Feel the knuckles, feel the shape of your hand and the fleshy part by your thumb and feel around your wrist. Do this for a few minutes and begin to feel the entire hand. Feel the blood circulating in it. Feel the tingling of life in your palm and in your hand.

If you can do this with a hand in a few minutes, what do you think will happen if you concentrate on your heart? Is it any different than bringing sensation to your hand? It has nothing to lose and nothing to reveal. So, make the same effort and begin to feel around your heart, and say inside, "Listen, it's you or me. I want you to open." You have to say, "I want to surrender, I want to open." When you hear a little tremor, begin to talk and say, "You have to open because I really want to live and have a spiritual life."

Do this for a couple of hours. You will cry, you will laugh, you will go through everything. Finally, you will begin to feel energy and this thing will crack and suddenly function consciously. And six months from now when you take a breath and feel life and love flowing out of it, you will know that it is a living organ. You will look at somebody you love and begin to feel this thing giving out a positive energy. Or you will wake up one morning with this thing as dead as a mackerel, and knowing that you are crazy, you will try to stay quiet that day. This is what the heart is about—to tell you consciously where you are or if you are functioning.

* * *

Without a heart, a person cannot have a spiritual life because the heart is where you go with your wish to grow. Without a heart, it is like peeing on a rock—it all runs off. You say, "I wish to grow, I wish to grow, so I'm growing." What kind of growing? This thing has to really open inside and begin to expand at your will and allow you to feel.

Hold your two hands together and become aware of the energy accumulating in them like a ball of fire. Feel all of your fingers and your palms as if you were holding snow and then begin to feel the energy coming between the wrists. This is exactly how the heart is shaped and how it functions. Feel this trembling on the outside and feel it from the middle where you are sucking energy into the center of the heart. The heart begins to open like a flower. To have a spiritual life or an ordinary life, to have any sense of people at all, takes practicing this. It's absolutely essential to feel this.

I go through this endlessly with every single student. You come in and I open regardless of whether I love you a little or a lot. I make this thing open—I make my heart function for you. I won't work with you unless I can serve you with this kind of equipment. And you must be able to serve the same way. I open my heart through the chakras and feel the energy coming down, bubbling in my sex organs, and rising up my spinal column to the top of my head. This gives me a fully equipped mechanism and I can work with you. But if you come to me and talk off the surface, how can I nourish you? How can I give you the connection that I'm trying to give? I work very deeply and very hard. I work individually with all of you and I want an effect. I want you to grow; this is the purpose of my life. From within yourself, you must open enough for me to get inside. But if you are closed tighter than a clam, I have to poke you here and there to find a place to stick in the knife. You don't make it easy for me.

I'm gone every weekend for two or three days traveling and teaching. I work sixteen-hour days besides coming back and earning my own living. And I'm glad to do it. But I want to work deeper with every one of you. I want you to grow in depth and commit yourself inside to this depth. If I talk to you this way, it is only because I love you. It kills me to see any human being express the limitation of his or her creative potential. God made us to have wonderful lives, to really grow and give life to other people. And the world is the way it is because people don't do it, because they are not functioning according to their capacity. Your capacity to say "I wish to grow" and have your heart open makes you grow more. And to be able to admit when you are expressing a limitation takes consciousness, not humility. It takes knowing the difference. If you don't know what it is to have a heart, then when your heart closes in a deep way to somebody, you won't recognize how you express yourself. And how can I not be patient with you or anyone else? You can't beat somebody for being ignorant.

I want you to grow because I won't be here next year. I will be away for six months and longer in the future. It is my need to fulfill what God has given me to do. It is not that I don't love you—because I love you very much. But if you grow, you will be sufficient. There is no reason that in six weeks every one of you cannot have a capacity to express your growth in being freer. You'll miss me, I'll miss you, but I really have to go other places. And there is a certain area of the world that I have to start visiting to do my work for my own evolvement. But there is no sense bringing you something else if you haven't the capacity to do these other things.

These are the treasures I want to give you—I'm not holding back. If I have an experience in the morning, I will give it to you an hour later. Or if I had it last night, I will give it to you today. It's not day-old bread, it's not year-old bread, and it's not anyone else's. It's my own living thing that I give you. It is fresh and you can take it inside. But you must have a mechanism that functions. Otherwise what good is it? If you can't sit here and consciously draw in this energy, your mechanism will not open in you the corresponding places. Take in the force that is coming through me so that your brain registers the entrance of a higher nature. It is a higher kind of food that your brain will attach to and begin sending a corresponding energy into your system on a permanent basis.

It's like getting an extra milk delivery in the morning. If your milkman sees two empty bottles on your doorstep, even though you only need one bottle, his brain says, "Wow, this person must have a new baby. I better leave two bottles every day." By drinking in the extra milk, you will expand your capacity and grow spiritually.

* * *

*R*egardless of how good the tire is, one hole will ruin it. You don't need a puncture in every chakra to be dead. A hole in any one of them is a blowout. It's true of every kind of thing that travels whether it's a spaceship or a balloon. Put a single hole through it and the whole thing is gone. And yet, while you think it will work one way or another—in reality the flow of energy must be connected. And it costs me. I really care more than you can believe and you have to open to that. You are not a herd of goats and I can't throw this one or that one out. I want to see every one of you grow, be free, and do what you want to do. I'm not trying to keep you.

I have traveled all over the world and know that, at best, you might get compassion from other teachers. Nobody, however, tells you that you have a chance. They have a chance but you're just out of luck. You can look at them and that's compensation enough. Horse feathers! You're here for one reason and one reason only—to grow and deeply express this growth in freedom and happiness, to experience your realization. Realization, realization, realization, realization, realization entering right into infinity. It is not limited realization. I want you to have this thing so that you understand it conceptually and practically. And if you drop dead when you are thirty or forty or fifty, die working so that you can come back and start this thing much earlier in a deep way.

Our spiritual work is simple. It is growing and saving your life energy every day and, in your deep unconsciousness, knowing that it is available for you. This is wished for you—and rarely do people have somebody in their lives wishing them to be free.

* * *

In spiritual work, there has to be a sense of joy as well as a sense of humor. Once you connect and begin to hear things in the atmosphere, for those beings on a higher level, you are just on closed-circuit television. They watch you facing life without a sponsor. They sit there and say, "Oh, there's Jack facing life, and there he goes—doing the same thing again." And they really set you up as some strange little creature going this way and that way, one not even as clever as a mouse who can ring a bell and get food. Look at this guy—he's repeating again. Just like a soap opera, it doesn't matter when they tune you in, night or day, you are doing the same little routine all the time.

It's ridiculous. I have seen this over and over. You think, "Oh, I'll never get anywhere—the odds are fifty-to-one." And I say, "Screw you, baby, I'm going to do it." If I do it, I will never have the lack of self-respect that allows myself to repeat endlessly a pattern that expresses a limitation of my energy. Because energy is God, and it's terrible to demean God. There is a real need for people to grow, to purify the earth's atmosphere, to show that it doesn't have to be a closed cup. It's like a smog that covers this earth, and somebody has to reach beyond it and bring a freshness to the atmosphere. It is essential. It is a life-giving energy. You can look at the kinds of situations that you feel your heart go out to, but nothing is more terrible than this limitation put on people. It is not your fault and it is not their fault. It is nobody's fault. You are only responsible when you have been given a concept that you refuse to respond to. But you have to feel in your heart that you really have this opportunity. If you ever have within you something that you can't accept or don't like, then you have the right to say no. But you are not doing well if you don't come and say, "Look, I don't understand this" or "I can't accept that."

I am perfectly willing to change. I have changed by demand and now I am here to serve you, not myself. I am here to break down in myself anything that is a problem for you in your ability to take energy from me. Understand that this is your right as a human being. The teacher is the servant. The teacher is not here to force you into anything. You serve not only by your ability to take the energy, but by speaking up consciously to demand more.

* * *

*T*ry to open and feel the flow of energy come through you and rise to the top of your head. Then as you do your meditation work, feel it expand. The chakra will grow from this internal feeding and go beyond the physical body to draw energy from the atmosphere. This life flow is what you can consciously bring through your body through the course of your breathing exercise. When you sit down and breathe, the energy comes down your front chakras and goes around to rise up your spine. This flow inside you feeds the chakras and allows them to slowly open like a seed beginning to sprout.

Our thirty-minute class provides more than enough energy because growth takes place at a particular rate. We can only assimilate so much energy at a time. And trying to do spiritual work fourteen hours a day is ridiculous. As you go through your day, take a breath every half hour and try to control the tensions that you give off. These tensions grind up and destroy any life force. They eat deeply into the energy of a human being. Just as if you drink orange juice and then smoke a cigarette, the vitamin C is destroyed.

So, try to act like a nice person even if you don't feel like one. Restrain yourself from getting mad because it takes so much energy. Control your mind and your emotions and let the energy begin to expand. Spiritual work must be done with consciousness.

CHAPTER 14

We have the capacity to see familiar patterns in our own and other people's lives. One way to begin understanding ourselves is by holding back and observing the changes and tensions other people experience. This allows us to begin seeing something that we should be able to see within ourselves. If we can watch somebody else react with a great deal of tension and unhappiness, we then have a clue that this is the nature of energy working in the atmosphere and one way that we react to that energy.

Often we get caught because of a similar pattern or similar tension in the atmosphere. We get caught because it is a reflection of ourselves in another person. Try to watch people as if you were watching a movie or television program. Look at them and see the way they work, watch the way they react to and interact with others. Among other things, you can't help but develop a sense of humor. Watching somebody else fumble a situation that you fumbled, and seeing them get mad or feel rejected the same way you did begins to show you how stupid and simple and finally how funny it really is. Because they do it and because you are here looking there, it is laughable. But when you do it, it becomes an insult. It affects your personality and is a healthy and a real way to learn. If you can laugh at somebody else, then you can begin to laugh at yourself.

* * *

*A*ll we do in our lives is fit pieces of a jigsaw puzzle in the wrong place. And there is nothing serious about that. It is just a question of having the detachment to see how bad the fit is or how bad the color match is. But our tensions blind us. It is the seriousness with which we handle something that makes it look like something else. Take away this blue thing and you find that it is green. Take away this brown thing and you see that it is purple or something far removed from reality. It is always the involvement, the fact that we carry the energy of one nature into another plane of existence, that limits our existence. We don't discriminate enough. So when we have a spiritual experience and try to bring it to the physical level, we lose it because it has a different density, a different color, and a different feel.

Life expresses our creative capacity to put our energy where it belongs, and we repeat patterns endlessly. We do the same thing over and over without success until we finally figure out that there is another way. We put ourselves through great torture fumbling our way through life—not because we enjoy the torture but because we hope somebody will take our hand and lead us. If we do attract a lot of help, we only become ineffective. We must work from our own muscles. It is not somebody else's good advice, it is our individual capacity to work, gather our own energy, and consciously do these things that make us stretch. This is how human beings develop capacity and creativity.

* * *

*I*t is your effectiveness that allows you to grow—not somebody else's. Sitting here with me is the same thing. The energy field is a little different. If you consciously drink in the energy, you will find your muscles restructure themselves into a different pattern. This is what you work for. You can take in a higher energy, absorb it consciously, bring it through you, and feed it to your muscles. When you leave, you can walk away, take a breath, and break down the molecular structure.

It is no different than people who are paralyzed. They work with their muscles daily to limber them to where eventually they can work in their ordinary way. Physically, you try to put energy inside muscles so that they can project a different pattern. This increases your energy and gives you the capacity to exhibit a different pattern. This happens continually. Spiritual work is only effective when it allows you to change patterns and raise the level of your consciousness.

At the same time, you must also consciously break down negative tensions. You wash out of yourself the tensions that bind you. They are a kind of arthritis that structures your muscles in a certain way. You have a much better chance if before you begin your breathing exercise, or when you get up in the morning, you take a breath, begin to feel the flow, and while you are taking a shower, you feel that you are washing away not only the dirt on your body but your resistance to change. You become more flexible so that as a situation arises and you begin to feel anger or despair, you can pull back and rise above it a little more each time. You can begin to see that the same situation offers alternatives—and this allows you to become free. Your concepts don't become horizontal, you acquire more intellectualism, you empty out internally, you reduce tensions, you reduce body poisons, you become elastic in a way that enables you to open inside and draw in energy more deeply and more effectively. You are energizing your system, drawing out of the atmosphere and out of life situations. This makes you aware of what gives you energy and life and turns you around inside. Otherwise you find yourself crawling along a life path of limited existence.

* * *

To limit yourself to this existence is to limit yourself to thousands of years and endless lifetimes because you are trying to fit into a pattern that somebody else devised. All religions and philosophies ultimately express the limitation of the moment. They are fine for stepping stones but they are not good as an expression of you. You have to be above something to encompass it within yourself, to really digest it and rise above it. I do not want my ideas or attitudes to limit you. To be truly nourished, you must throw off any bones, gristle, or other limitations that exist within the concept for your own personal growth. Taking in the nourishment is wonderful, but you must rise with it to a place that can free you—not bind you.

Live with the energy on an abstract level and don't get caught up by my personality, form, or words. Drink in the energy strictly as energy and feel it connect inside. Nothing in me wants to limit you to my plane of existence. I am only giving you nourishment to draw from that allows you to feel your own connection. The energy sets up different patterns in every person. The patterns are the lines through which the energy comes. Take it in, incorporate it into your being, and rise above the connection so that you aren't restricted or crystallized. I don't want to be carrying you in my arms ten years or five years from now. Work for your own freedom and feel this with every human being.

We have an incredible capacity to want to embrace everybody and everything because we lack the courage within ourselves to grow. This has nothing to do with spirituality. This has to do with someone becoming the parasite of another human being. To become free is to draw in the energy as nourishment. Feel it as you breathe deeply inside. Feel it in your sex organs as a pulsation and vitality. Then as the energy comes up your spinal column, feel the burning as it is incorporated in you as food and works as a catalyst. As you absorb it, congestion and limitation are burned away.

* * *

The real purpose of a spiritual feeding is not to glue you forever to a place where you feel comfortable. It is to unglue you, to soak you free of old patterns, and to allow you to develop muscles by deeply drawing in nourishment and feeling the breakup inside. You have a sense of your muscles spreading out to become a root system that draws more and more energy. It is not a mother, father, sister, brother, husband, lover, or any other relationship. It is a relationship that draws in you something that destroys the limitation of yourself and allows you to become free and to stay free. When you get crapped up in your mind or your emotions or anything else, it is only your limitation. I certainly don't want that. That I feel for you and with you and that I love you goes without saying. This is how I can draw energy from you to use for my own growth. The only way I can be free is to pour back into you an energy that refines what I take and allows you to grow. And as you grow, you should become consciously detached—not attached. Just as when milking a cow, you don't stand in a place where you get kicked in the guts, you stand a little to the side and milk consciously. Coming close enough to get kicked is your limitation. It is your expression of wanting to be smacked because you don't have the sense to move a little to the right or a little to the left.

The most important thing is that when you do take it, be sure to hold onto it. A lot of you are remiss in that. You are so open and emotional and involved that when you leave, the energy pours out of you like spilt milk. Remember—taking is less than half of any spiritual exercise. You must have the ability to retain the energy inside and keep taking.

* * *

I used to sit in school and finish my work and like a beggar run behind people and collect the bits and pieces that overflowed from their creative capacity. Whatever they took, they lost some, and I would go behind and pick it up. And I would follow a horse and pick up the droppings if it really served my purpose. You must realize that the energy is not just mine or hers or his—the atmosphere around you is yours, too. Everyone gathers whatever energy is available. And if they throw it away, you can pick it up. You can sit there and let them spill out their guts to you. Stay quiet and just drink it in. Don't get involved and react. If you do, you just throw your energy into the void with theirs. By standing up from your meditation and immediately talking or spewing tensions, you lose whatever you just gained. Have the awareness and capacity to retain what you receive.

I used to walk around in the halls and not look to the right or left. I wouldn't listen to anybody. Everything would go in one ear and out the other. And I've got a big mouth. I make a lot of noise and am very emotional. But I can do all of these things after I completely absorb the spirituality that I am involved with. Whether I am playing poker or talking, I am making every effort to gather within myself the energy of that moment. I am trying to open and relate and feel in all of you this flow of energy in a conscious way. I live to grow so that you can do the same thing.

You can be involved on this level and consciously store up the energy by being a little detached. You are capable of bringing this energy down through you and up your spinal column. There is nothing wrong in it. In fact, it is wrong to not do it. *Trying* to be involved has no meaning whatsoever—you have to be consciously involved. Understand that being involved in life is the nature of a human being who has no discipline or control. We get caught endlessly because we can't retain the connection between ourselves and life and between ourselves and our spiritual growth.

* * *

I had a store full of people the other day—and when an accident occurred in front of the store, everyone ran out. I would never run out to an accident. Why follow a crowd of five hundred people pouring their energy into the atmosphere? Instead I sat very quietly and absorbed what was being dropped around me in the store. It is people's false sense of being humanitarian. If somebody took out a pad and pencil and asked for the names of those who saw the accident, everyone would run for their lives. It is a false sense of drama. There is nothing more dramatic than sitting in the middle of that stupidity and absorbing the energy and the atmosphere and rising above it. It is extraordinary to watch people doing all kinds of numbers that have nothing to do with what is taking place. It is their expression of drama.

You find the same thing if you go to a funeral and watch people acting out what they think they should be doing. To see genuine emotion in a deep way is rare. Because if you really love somebody who has lost their physical life, the only thing to do is to sit and love that person. His or her seed is going to another dimension and should be surrounded by love and nourishment, not by crying and holding on. Allow this seed to leave full of positive feelings and energy. Otherwise you are using the person to satisfy your own limitation and inability to live. People go because we wear them out. They have fulfilled their purpose and the only thing we can do is send them a box of cookies and a bouquet of flowers from our hearts. The nourishment they require now is on another level.

Carry your spiritual life into the world. You can become detached and involved with your evolvement and simultaneously see life from a higher and higher place.

* * *

*R*emarkable spiritual things have been happening to me this week. It has been accompanied by lousy business at my antique store and lousy feelings—but they go together. This spiritual depth is involved in cleaning me out and preparing me for the change that will take place in my life. Of this, you have to be conscious. To get results, your mechanism has to be cleaned out occasionally. Give it a chance to be scrubbed and burnished and refurbished and oiled to bring it up to a higher level of productivity. When we feel these spiritual operations begin, we have to detach gratefully from some things that aren't essential and allow these processes to take place inside. If life is trying to help you detach and increase your spiritual capacity, and you keep running away because you are insecure—you can't stand a week without business or a day without some return for your mind or emotions—then you only reduce the chance for these higher forces to take you to a higher place.

* * *

*S*tudent: In the business world, should I look for more responsibilities?

Rudi: Yes, you should look for more of everything, but you should also look for more consciousness. If you build something bigger here, it should bring more balance there. We can't get lost in one thing. We have to be lost in everything and detached from everything. Strengthening ourselves in one area should simultaneously strengthen us in all others. Only a limited focus prevents us from seeing life fully. We look at one thing, become fascinated by it, and lose sight of the rest of our lives.

There's a balance in life. Your ability to see it makes you responsible for it. This is business. This is your home. This is your spiritual life. This is whatever other life you have. If you don't see them all simultaneously, one area will grow and completely overpower the overall logistics of your life. By focusing too strongly in any one direction—even a spiritual direction—you lose a sense of reality and balance. If all you do is meditate, what happens? You get thrown out of your house for not paying rent and have to spend the next six weeks running around like a maniac. Any spiritual growth you had is ground away. Being conscious of everything represents your capacity to utilize any gift that you receive. You will lack the energy to sustain what you build unless you are effective in every area of your life. Everything should support your growth—otherwise it is an illusion.

* * *

*I*f Spinoza says something is great, it's great. If Krishna says so, it's also great. If our mother says it's stupid, we don't listen.

God speaks in many different ways. We must learn to not identify with the speaker so we can hear. There is a simple logic to life. And we can learn from it because it talks all the time. But we wait for it to look a certain way before we listen. And then we get stung and we look back and say, "Oh, blah, blah, blah . . ." It's like having somebody who you don't consider a good friend tell you something that your "good" friend said about you. You don't accept it because you don't like the person who gave you the good advice. You immediately disqualify it. We pick and choose based on personality—not based on logic and certainly not based on consciousness.

* * *

Don't identify with what goes on in your mind during meditation. There is nothing to identify with. Once I gave a two-hour class while an entire musical comedy danced in my brain. And they even wore better costumes than when I saw the show on Broadway. Just let it go. It has nothing to do with anything. It is just another kind of nuisance. By paying attention to it, it will go through every repertoire that ever existed. By forgetting it, it won't bother you. It is trying to catch you. It is your consciousness testing to see whether you get involved or not. And why should it let the treasures that exist emerge if you are the kind of fool who will get involved in this? It is testing you.

No court or judge in the world is as strong as those sitting inside of you. They hand you very strict sentences. We do this to ourselves continually because it is our own creativity that is locked underneath the tension and ignorance we have accumulated in this life. If we can quiet ourselves down, relax, take the energy that's given us and use it, then we can throw off the tensions and begin to see little treasures that start to shine. We begin to understand what life is all about.

* * *

We are each possessed by a fool. We are possessed by the most stupid thing that exists—our superficial selves. And living underneath are many bright, creative beings who manifest problems to test the fool.

Our past creative capacity represents thousands or maybe millions of years. And they say, "Let's see what you do with it." And if you treat it with respect and begin to make something out of it, these inner beings will remove one layer and then another layer and another.

This treasure exists in every human being. It is a treasure of consciousness and spirituality and every kind of capacity. And it comes out strongly. Maybe just a little part of it will be seen in you. So you get a form that says: "You have the capacity to tell fortunes or read astrology." And you take this slip and make this your spiritual life instead of continuing to release the treasure that exists inside. All of you represent the first couple of inches of what exists inside me. And I intend to live completely all of the fabric that exists inside me. I want to use it up because I want to be finished. For you to come to this creative depth means you can't not have the guts to be used up this way. Otherwise, you are like a miser hoarding this treasure so that when you die, you can take it with you. And when people say you can't take it with you, it's untrue. People die and take with them their internal buried treasure. They carry it from lifetime to lifetime to lifetime. It is the most cursed treasure of all because you never reap its reward. You can never spend it.

But I'm beginning to really enjoy spending the treasure inside me. I'm going to blow every penny before I'm finished because all I want in this life is to get rid of everything. All my accumulated love and knowledge is going out and continues to go out. I want to be empty. I want to give back everything. And you can do this, too. You just need guts. In the depth of your unconscious, to let the real thing inside you start to come to the surface takes guts and a sincere desire to connect with it.

This is why you can take something from me and grow. I am taking it out of a million years of creativity and spirituality. You can have as much of it as you want because I absolutely don't want it. I'm glad to give it away. You can take based on your own intelligence and your own capacity. You can sit and just wind it up inside you. You can get just as much sitting there and unwinding me in you. It is very, very simple. I have had it with other people. I got it from Nityananda that way. I got it from the Shankaracharya of Puri that way. I've filled myself and filled myself and filled myself. But I needed their consent to really let me grow. This is the reason for taking from me or someone else. Not that what somebody has is good—because it's not. The goal is to be reduced to the energy that allows you to begin loosening up your inner treasure. By working spiritually, you draw this energy around just like an enormous cocoon. As you unwind from inside you, this thing begins to show on the out-side—this spirituality, this aura, this atmosphere, this con-sciousness. You are taking from inside the cocoon and unwinding it. And the only way it can be unwound is to give it away.

So, I'm giving mine away—and you are very wel-come to it. If you take it and bind yourself with it, then you are the worst fool in existence. It should not be taken as a solid, but rather as a very light energy to set you free in yourself. I don't want to bind you with my ideas and my limitations. Reduce it to an energy that can free you and unwind the congestion within you.

And truly I say this with love—as I learn, I give to you. I haven't the capacity to hold back a fourth or a third or a drop of the energy because I really want out. And the only time you can get from anybody is when they are going out of business. And I've been having a going-out-of-business sale these last couple of years. So you can get bargains based on the intelligence within yourself. It's the old story again. During the Depression, they said somebody wasn't doing well and then set the factory on fire. Well, this is exactly what I am doing because I don't want this factory to exist much longer. But don't worry, I have insurance.

CHAPTER 15

You are responsible for your spiritual practice and for your connection with me. When you sit in meditation, don't be like an animal in its nest wiggling around trying to find the usual comfortable spot—and don't look for the place inside that worked for you yesterday. Sit down working deeply. Open and reach for a higher connection because I don't want to feel the old one any more than I care to eat something that was cooked three days ago and reheated. Our connection should represent a freshness, a vitality, and a sense of creation and potential for each other's realization—not a complacency or the attainment of a satisfactory level. It's like adequate heating or adequate wiring. It may be sufficient for our immediate needs, but it doesn't allow for the enormous change that should take place.

* * *

I am grateful because I feel this love flowing out of my heart and a maturity in me that can feed and nourish all of you. Throughout my body I begin to experience these things. And when you open deeper, this nourishment will come in and open in you as it has in me. We grow only from the nature of what we are fed. This deeper feeding and more refined energy express creation reaching a higher level—and it can be given and exchanged. If you take and grow from that, you work from a higher place in yourself. Basically, when we work, we are working for the atmosphere. Only the people we relate to give us something to focus on and it is less than what we put out in the atmosphere. We actually put out much more nourishment than is used by the people we relate to.

We refine the atmosphere around us and serve God in the deepest sense. It is not an eclectic thing of working and knowing. Rather we work and grow and don't know because to know is to express the limitation of the moment. To allow yourself the freedom to not know or to not understand now and to be grateful for living and growing represents a freedom that transcends any truth or knowledge. Every truth and every piece of knowledge is the limitation of people who could not go further. And so they say, "This is it," and the "it" is their limitation. It needn't be your limitation. You really have to breathe and open and deeply feel the flow of your creative energy passing through and feeding every part of your body. Expand and feel the sweetness in your heart. Feel the gratitude for the expression of your growth. Feeling this flow of energy, you also become free. You can open more and start to draw more slowly from the actual atmosphere, not just from people. Your muscles and the root system within you are taking in energy and can reach into the cosmos. They are not limited to this one plane of existence.

The concept of God or paradise or whatever you wish to call it simply expresses a higher plane of creative

energy. Many schools of philosophy and religion express
it as being on the earth. And it is on the earth. It is reaching from within yourself to draw down, open, and take in
this higher energy. You all sit in this little circle of your
own atmosphere. If you only think of an area of six or
eight inches, then this is the entire atmosphere you live in.
But if you reach out another two feet, you will be in another dimension. With consciousness, you are capable of this.

When you open in yourself, you not only feel the
om sound coming in, but from your heart you can feel and
bring inside something as far as your fingers can reach.
You can begin relating to a finer atmosphere with a different density and a different kind of molecular structure. You
can feel the lightness inside as you draw from that, and if
you can visualize another area twice as far away and a
level above that, you can begin to consciously allow the
nourishment from these areas to enter you and make a
connection. This connection then gives you a root system
that can reach from one dimension to another. Human
beings who wish to experience consciousness must have
inside themselves these different muscles reaching into
many different dimensions simultaneously. It isn't to reach
from here to paradise—it is to reach from one dimension to
another and to another and another. This gives you the
nourishment to feed the structure within you that internal-
ly represents the equation that exists outside.

* * *

A tree's rings denote good years and bad years.
Within ourselves, different circles represent dimensions

that, were we to cut them in half, would enable us to see which was a good growing year and which was a poor growing year. Human beings have within their structures visible selves as well as many invisible selves. These parts of you can be given nourishment and can express creativity and growth. But as you make an effort, as you do your breathing exercise, and as you relate to yourself consciously, you must not think of yourself as somebody simply doing this work. You should reach beyond it every day and not just make the effort that you are responsible for. You should open beyond it so that you are not limited to the atmosphere of a day.

If your concept is to do more than you are responsible for, your relationships with other people deepen. You will open and see and feel and begin to understand that the person you look at can change, if you change your attitude about them. The Biblical idea of turning the other cheek refers to someone with the detachment to not need to react to a violent act. You can open and look and understand and behave in a way that instead of shutting somebody off from you really opens them and allows them to come closer. We constantly justify the acts we do by the acts we see and our projection of a person. But it is wrong to limit somebody because of your prejudice, because of your attitude, and because of what you see and feel. It does nothing except limit you to a dimension.

If you can surrender, if you can breathe, draw in your energy, and become a little more detached, you begin to open a universe of new potential, a universe of alternatives that you can use and function with. You can be different, and within this energy field of alternatives you can also offer somebody an alternative—which is certainly a better thing than threatening or fighting. Instead of using one level and one dimension of energy, you open and expand to another within which there is an alternative. There is love and energy and consciousness. And what is it when we say we love somebody? It means that instead of eating them alive and suffocating them, we can move back a step, open, and take in their love and energy.

* * *

You can't eat my energy. It's impossible. You can only use it, one on one with whatever you take in from the atmosphere around you. Because no energy from any human being, regardless of whether it's me or God, is assimilable. You can only assimilate someone else's creative energy based on the amount you encompass outside. So if you open to me and you open inside yourself at the same time, you drink in me and that energy. It becomes a marriage of energies. By being on top of somebody like a parasite, there is only tension. You suck out their energy and waste it. It goes right through the body because it is done emotionally—not consciously.

Consciousness has to do with detachment. If your spiritual work is not done with detachment, you will never be able to take from anybody and assimilate it in your body. Regardless of how fanatical you might be, you will never be realized. It must be fanaticism with consciousness. It must be emotion with detachment. It must also be a wish with detachment. Because no human being can take in something different from itself, you must draw in at least equally from an outside force that you wish to take from. It will not adjust to the appetite of a body. It is this mixture of detachment and objective which you draw from somebody that you can bring inside yourself. This is the only way the body can assimilate.

I know that with every test I faced in my life, I was able to keep a distance between myself and the test. I was able to remain conscious of the separation that enabled the change to be assimilated within me. This is the thing that destroys more people because they think that this zest, this violence, this need expresses something. But it only expresses the ability to burn up. To burn and grow and feed and nourish is what we are here for. Your garbage burns but the energy that you take from me, the energy that you draw from the atmosphere has to be absorbed in a solution that has to do with your atmosphere and a change. Only then can this thing come inside and grow in a real way.

* * *

You absorb spiritual energy the same way you eat roast beef. Roast beef is heavy. So, you eat it with a salad, you eat it with vegetables, you eat it with bread and butter. They thin it out and make it easier for your body to take and assimilate. If you just ate chunks of roast beef, what would happen? You'd get constipated, right? Well, creative energy is a very strong force. It's a hundred times stronger than roast beef. It's like eating liver pâté. Pâté is very strong—it's made to put on crackers. So, too, is spirit. While spiritual energy is a light energy, it is also a very deep and very dense energy. It needs assimilation. It needs conscious balancing—twenty-four hours of consciousness and twenty minutes of spirituality. But if you try to work and even succeed in connecting to spiritual energy alone, you would burn out or freak out. It would be impossible. People drive themselves crazy by overdoing.

Spiritual energy is a concentrate. By assimilating a combination of your own energy and a little bit of spiritual energy, you are able to assimilate it. I have a statue of Nityananda upstairs and I look at it for one minute a day. I feel that worship in me all the time. And because I have the ability to draw into myself on another level, I have Nityananda on a spiritual level. This is a cosmic statue that was made for our advanced work. The energy is so concentrated that a person just needs a little bit. There will always be fools who come and sit there and burn themselves to a crust trying to open. It's very powerful. All you need is twenty-four hours a day away from and two minutes in front of this statue. But it is the nature of people to go before something very powerful, open completely, draw it into themselves, and then have to go into a corner to recover for thirty-five years.

* * *

Spiritual energy is extraordinarily strong. The consciousness with which you draw it in, the depth to which you draw it, and your consciousness during the day allows it to be assimilated. You work for half an hour a day but you are aware of it. You feel the flow through you all day long and absorb it. It's just like absorbing food. You eat, you digest, and then you get rid of what you can't digest. You take consciously, you absorb consciously, you get rid of consciously—just like a bowel movement. Every day for a few minutes, you have to take a deep breath and flush out the negative psychic tension that exists. Otherwise how can you change? You're feeding something, it expands, and then it comes back again.

You have to expand and drop some of the thicker energy that can't be absorbed. Then you grow. Otherwise, you expand on the life level, you contract, you expand a little more and a little more. What happens? You become very successful in life. But our work is not to become successful in life—it is to evolve successfully toward our objective, which is to be free and to have realization. Realization must take place every single day. There is no such a thing as a sudden clap of lightning giving somebody realization. They always think, well, it doesn't matter because one day it's going to strike. Realization doesn't strike that way. It slowly builds up, builds up, builds up, builds up—like an inverted pyramid expanding a little more every day.

Understand that when you raise the level of energy, you automatically have to change the mechanism. After changing your mechanism, you consciously have to reach for a deeper energy so that the mechanism can run in a deeper and more conscious way.

* * *

In a real sense, spiritual work manifests when you increase your energy. You should wake up at night in your sleep and feel that somebody is working in you. You feel your wiring being changed, things touching your heart, something opening your brain. It is a spiritual dimension that expresses itself with experience. I mean, I had thousands and thousands of operations where I used to wake up at night and—clink, clink, clink, clink—little steel instruments hitting each other, like Con Edison's

"Work We Must." This went on and on and I got so sick and tired of smelling formaldehyde and feeling bandages on my head and hearing the clink clink of the instruments and having that light in my face. It made me sick to my stomach. But it went on, and this is a reality.

It is not a fable. It is not an illusion. It is the reality of changing the nature in a human being. You are being changed because you have increased the level of your energy and you should submit as consciously and as gracefully as you can. It's like hearing the garbage cans rattle at four in the morning. Clink, clink, clink, clink, clink, and you have more energy. You attract a higher level that is outfitting your insides with the ability to go the next step. Look at people and begin to understand the low level this life is for most people. The deadness, the thickness that's involved in it—there is no refining of their mechanisms. There may be a refining of culture and other outer things, but the inner thing does not exist for them. Basically, when you look at people you find that they are not happy, they are not deeply satisfied, and there is no flow between you and them.

You may find a woman or a man as refined as a Swiss clock. But when you look inside, there is nothing humming. The only way to have the vitality to experience in depth what you are responsible for and can attract is by breathing, holding your breath inside until you feel an expansion take place, and feeling your life flow. As it increases, this life flow inside you feeds the chakras. The chakras, in turn, give off a chemistry as they change, emitting from inside them a necessary chemistry. This unifies and begins to change your mechanism. You do not have a spiritual life until you go through these changes and begin to see and hear them.

* * *

I came out of the army with a lesion in my leg and fifteen doctors poking and pulling me, putting this thing and that thing on it. And so when I came back to New York, I went to Mt. Sinai Hospital because another lesion was coming out, but the original specimen was so destroyed they couldn't tell what it was anymore. The doctor at Mt. Sinai was very happy about it and said to let it grow. And I told him to take it off and stick it on his child's leg and watch what happened because I wasn't going to develop this thing for somebody else to study. So it was removed and I never knew what it was. I was spared the drama.

I don't have to know those things, and neither do you. But what you should know is that you have an opportunity that will never again exist in your life. What we have here is remarkable in its capacity to grow and express. This is really what the Aquarian Age represents. It is a level and a dimension and a drama that is wonderful. And to really have guts doesn't mean that you will not be afraid. When the Bible says that you will walk through the valley of the shadow of death and fear no evil, it doesn't mean that you aren't afraid. It means that you have to overcome the terror in your mind. And if you take a breath and say, "Am I going to sit here and watch—or do?" you just shut up, keep walking, and do your breathing exercise.

It takes guts to live. It doesn't mean that you aren't afraid. It doesn't mean that you don't have pangs in your heart. It means that you have the guts to keep moving—and then not only will your stupidity and fear drop away, but you will grow in a very deep way. This is not something I'm trying to drop on you. It's something I've worked out in my own little home laboratory a million times. I never give an exercise until I've practiced it over and over and over. And the test for anything is when you go home and make a deeper commitment to yourself. You find your unconscious, this thing deep inside you that constitutes ninety-nine percent of your life that you never reach into. And when you reach into it, you say, "Look, I am about to embark on something, please open for me, let me find the chemistry, let me find the depth to really grow and have a spiritual life. I really wish to grow, I really want to commit myself." You feel your heart open and you feel something else open. And along with it will rise the chemistry and the energy that's needed.

This is all your commitment is. It's not to follow me or anyone else around the block. It's your commitment to yourself for your own creative potential, for your own evolvement, for your own freedom. Don't commit yourself to me, I don't need that. Be committed to yourself and to your own potential. Ask and try to feel this flow increase within you. Inside, try to feel the ability to breathe. Nourish your muscles with this breath and allow them to open.

* * *

I walked around Greenwich Village when I was twenty-five years old as if someone was pulling me by the nose. This thing pulled me and I walked through like someone in a deep sleep. My heart was breaking but I had no control. I begged inside and I spoke a thousand times a day to God, "Please, anything, but let me at least have some sense of control and some sense of dignity." I had no emotional control. I had no mental control. I had nothing. And I studied and worked and worked and worked and worked.

Slowly but surely you break through these things and emerge as a human being. This is what you have to see in yourself—that in some places, you're a dead goose. If somebody says a couple of key words you might as well jump out of the window because you are vulnerable. Whether it's greed or sexuality or your sense of power, that vulnerability is the thing that eats up and destroys your entire life. You have to be willing to open and surrender and really want to be a free human being. Then if life ends up giving you a piece of toast with butter and a glass of water or tea, that will be enough.

I swear to you that if everything around me disappeared tomorrow, I would walk away happy without a question because life has given me tremendously. I don't like working as hard as I do. But because of what is coming out of me and out of you, I am living a responsibility to God. If they took it away and said, "Okay, you're free now," I would go and live by the beach. I would eat clams. I probably would never look at another human being as long as I live because I would have worked myself free.

Find in yourself the ability to surrender and become freer and freer and freer. I know all of the five-star movies and the millions of people that my life will be composed of and I am not concerned. It is just a manifestation of the energy coming through me. It doesn't matter to me because it just means that I have to wash so much more vomit off the floor and wash so many more diapers, and I'm grateful for that. What I am doing is fulfilling the work that was given me.

I am not God. I am working and I am grateful to do a job. And when I'm tired, I hit my head on the floor a little bit, even today, and look around and realize that I am not what I was when I was twenty-five, twenty-seven, twenty-eight, twenty-nine, thirty years old—all the way up to the present moment. I am grateful every day for the evolving freedom and capacity to pull away from my tensions and for the ability to be so grateful to some of you for being here. I do not take any of you for granted. For what you mean to me, I am very grateful in my heart and soul, more than you can afford to believe. Some of you haven't the ego to feel value, and if I didn't feel that, you would not be here. Because I have used every one of you well and deeply, I feel the need to give you in return. As much as you need me, I need every single one of you or you would not be here. This is a two-way street and I am very grateful. I may make a little noise once in a while but that's only my stupidity.

* * *

*I*t is your right to take, it is your right to open, it is your right to draw through me the nourishment that you need—until you are able to draw on these other levels on your own. I require nothing in return. I appreciate it when somebody brings me flowers, but what I really need is your growth as my evolvement takes place. I need to work much more, I need you to work more, I need you to find a need inside to ask questions in depth. And I certainly need to get the hell out of here when it's all over with, and that's what I'm working for.

There's not a day in my life that I wouldn't be happy to take off my little finger if I could die on the spot and not leave any of you less than where you are. My life means absolutely nothing to me that way. That's why I can work this hard and this is what we should be working toward—to be free of all of this. To watch your paranoia disappear, to watch your fantasies disappear, to watch your simplicity and gratitude increase, to watch your loyalty grow to the people in your life, to feel love in a simple and wonderful way—these are the things that make it possible and worthwhile. If nobody else in the world loves you, you can come here and I love you. Understand that I need you and this is the real reflection of love. It is based on respect and growth.

* * *

*T*here is always turmoil when the energy in the atmosphere increases. And so, whatever you feel, don't think it is your limitation. You are being used and in return you have the right to use the energy that's there. Open, and if you feel crazy, go deeper and draw and draw and draw and draw until you get beneath it. In this way, you can draw in this energy and assimilate and grow. There's no reason to fall every time beneath tension or limitation. Take the energy and use it.

CHAPTER 16

With a spiritual practice, it only takes a few weeks before people forget why they started. They forget that their dedication is supposed to be permanent. And after working for a year or two, they start thinking of themselves as teachers or experts. And this is the greatest of all stupidities because these people stop having a greater spiritual life and start talking about things they know nothing about. You see this all the time in marriage and friendship where one party feels that something is more important than the relationship.

A spiritual practice cannot be maintained through neglect. It cannot be a secondary part of your life. Because you have a chance to go to a movie or to the theater, don't try to rush your spiritual life. It must be your primary reason for living. Don't fault lesser situations or the people you say you love. If you cannot open to this higher state, then most likely you are not open to anything. You are choking and destroying others by denying your ultimate potential. Keep your wish to grow spiritually and develop the capacity to stick to it—only then will you be free.

* * *

Growing in no way exonerates you from responsibility for your attitude and your direction. To not be open and have a flow inside that allows you to transcend the ordinary in a situation in no way justifies your living. It has nothing to do with reality. Instead you get caught up in the tensions and the emotions of the day and completely forget that a spiritual life is a higher and finer thing.

We continually have to make judgments. We continually have to work. And it's a simple thing of just taking a breath, feeling the energy come inside, and then rising above everything, whatever has caught us. It's the simplest thing in the world—it doesn't require even intelligence. But to see people with intelligence and capacity lose their direction every single day is appalling. And this goes on and on.

You see people who make a commitment to spiritual work, and yet they can't even remember to take a breath in the morning when brushing their teeth. If they remembered, they could wash their mouths with greater consciousness, realizing that they are ridding themselves of poisons. They could take a shower with the thought that they're not just physical functions. They are trying to cleanse themselves in order to become a vessel through which a higher force can flow. This is living consciously—and only consciously can we reach these deep forces that hold our bodies and minds and stop us from functioning emotionally and physically and every other way.

We get caught up in the emotions and the ideas and all the thoughts we think are so brilliant. Meanwhile we haven't really flushed the toilet in our psyche, in our hearts, and in our souls. We live with this filth day by day and become ground down by it. We become oppressive to the people we love because we can't make a very simple, conscious effort. And nothing in the world justifies that. I mean, there certainly are times when we can go through a crisis. However, we can go through the crisis working in a state of surrender. Then if we're tortured and things go on that we can't get rid of, fine. It's understandable. At least we're on a higher level. At least as we burn and as we are washed through, these lesser things can fall away. But sitting in a bathtub of our own filth and splashing around and talking and complaining has nothing to do with having a spiritual life. It has to do with the abysmal stupidity to forget that we have a consciousness by which we rise above it all.

* * *

Our ability to consciously rise regardless of our state at the moment is what makes a growing human being. It is consciousness that allows the energy to become something positive. Consciousness allows us to assimilate the growth or change so that it doesn't lay in one area of us to become a restriction or limitation. Consciousness allows our entire system to drink in the energy change and surrender the negative psychic tensions. If we have an incredible experience or go through a tremendous shock and don't do this negative psychic tension exercise, then we're stupid—because we work from one level to another, we rip it apart, we suffer with it, we go through all this agony, and it's like millions of molecules torn loose. If we don't do anything, we pay the price. Four days later this thing solidifies again and becomes exactly what it was.

There is no such thing as growth without breaking down the by-products. It should be growth that has been digested and allows the breaking down of energy and chemistry so that you can wash yourself out. Just as after you eat food, you wash out the poisons, psychically you wash out through any creative process the unassimilated energy so that you grow back in a different way. You are a changing human being. Without consciously ridding yourself of some of your chemistry every day, you will never change. Your mind will be fanciful, you will have illusions, but you will not be a human being undergoing a creative and spiritual change.

* * *

Student: How do you deal with tensions that arise during times of change?

Rudi: Tension is very strong energy that as you breathe deeply you can draw inside. You can suck the life energy out of tension. What you can't suck out, you should drop out several times a day. Just as when you eat food, you digest what you can and eliminate the by-products. The only way you can grow consciously is to eat the tensions of the day and allow the rest to fall away. In this way, you become compact and strong.

As you grow and consciously assimilate the energy in the flow of your life force, you build a strong internal mechanism. You replace your internal wigwam with a skyscraper. You put in a compressor and an extractor and start building all kinds of machinery inside. You install wiring and a sewer, everything you need to let your structure grow. Once this structure is finished, it demands another chemistry. This process is about growth—and growth brings new energy. The new energy destroys the old structure and creates a new mechanism. This new mechanism gathers the new energy and the new energy rises once again and spreads out on a new level. This cycle of death and rebirth we should be grateful for every day. We should be grateful that we can live and die and be reborn over and over and over.

Karma only limits spiritual morons who try to justify their existence by having somebody predict what you can or cannot do. Our ancestors took crude oil and rubbed it over their faces. Today we use it to heat our houses and for countless other things. This has to do with the ability of the mechanism over time to refine any product and broaden its capacity. Spiritually, you go through a generator that opens up your raw material. If you don't use the raw material, you become impoverished. If you use it, you develop the capacity to open more and more and more.

* * *

Coming back from Atlanta, I was sitting on the plane next to a very little old lady who had one hand bandaged and the other covered up with a knit glove. We started to talk and she said how she really dreaded coming East because she lived in the South and the last time she came back it was after being in a sixty-three-day coma. When she awoke she saw that her body had turned black because her system was dying. It eventually revived everywhere except in her fingers and she cried, she said, because every couple of days another finger fell off. And she asked if she might show me her hand. She said the last time she made this trip she came up to bury her father who lived in Big Indian, New York, and while she was there, her husband died in Georgia and she had to come back to bury him. That was a few weeks ago, and now she was returning to see her mother who would not be around much longer.

When you see how a person like this talks and faces life, that she can even share such a thing and be open, it makes us deeply ashamed of how we face the difficulties in our own lives. And I looked at her and was amazed to see the openness with which she treated it. And she said she was getting a little tired and would I order her a bourbon and water. I loved it. We talked a little more and I said, "You know, I may sound stupid, but I feel that you will have a very good life at the end of this year." And she said, "Funny you say that. I just had my astrology chart done and it said that in December my life would pick up."

Well, it had to. I mean, where could you go from there? That a person in this condition could have a positive attitude means that there is absolutely no justification for any of us to not look at life and be deeply grateful for what we have. This woman had one withered hand, and on the other one the fingers were already gone, and I said, "Can I carry your things." And she said, "You have your own bag." And I thought how ridiculous life is—another person would have answered yes even if you had fifteen bags hanging between your teeth. This is the difference with someone who has suffered, who understands life, and who has given of herself. She obviously was going to miss her connection because we had been two hours late departing and two hours late arriving, and yet she was quiet. She had enough quality to not make life difficult for anyone around her. She wasn't demanding special attention. The airline had a wheelchair waiting and I walked with her—no stuff, no noise, no anything.

We must begin to see that life is difficult for every single human being. It's rare to find someone who walks through it without problems. And if we can stop identifying with ourselves, we can understand that there are people who can help, people who you can open to, people who you can look to with respect, people who you can honor because of the way they live their lives. And these are people who don't come to a yoga class and who aren't exposed to a teacher who can help. This woman has nobody to give her what you can get here.

You can open inside. You have the ability to ask deeply to open and to grow. It is a simple thing of taking a breath and bringing your attention inside. Everything that happens in your head does nothing but give you a headache. It doesn't help you. So relax your shoulders and draw the energy from your mind into your heart and feel the joy of being alive.

* * *

The place we have in Georgia is a defunct Civil War-era plantation, and the twenty-odd rooms are half the size of our classroom in Manhattan. The students live there on two hundred and fifty dollars a month apiece and the place costs half a million bucks. They're waiting for the town of Athens to spread out and make it a subdivision. And in one six-window room, they had six and a half different kinds of drapes hanging. It was amazing how simply they lived. They had no money and they talked about having to lay in provisions because I was coming to visit. They had a tiny bowl of salad waiting for me and soybeans and so forth. Despite the lack of money, there was no poverty of soul, there was no poverty of attitude, and there certainly was no poverty of spirit. There was no heat and it was as cold as it is in New York, and it was wonderful because they gave everything they had with love. I was very happy. I took my shower and it was cold in the room and I thought that I would feel it—but the only thing I felt was the goodness of these twenty people who I found so easy to love.

It didn't matter that there was some dirt in the corner of the room because the real richness was inside. You don't correct somebody by ripping them to pieces and nagging them. By loving them they will grow and take care of these things in time. And their biggest worry—I mean, this house had more stuff laying around than you can believe—was that the landlord had promised that by tomorrow there would be new linoleum in the kitchen. The house needed six million other things, believe me, but they kept talking about this linoleum floor in the kitchen and it was wonderful. They were oblivious of the six million other things.

You all have to live this way in yourself. Take with gratitude what is available and don't continually attack everything like a neurotic person without the capacity to be happy. Feel the joy that is available at the moment in the atmosphere and in the people you are with. That will give you enlightenment for today.

* * *

*I*f we don't begin to see in our lives the things that are wonderful, nothing will ever happen. It is the collectiveness of the energy and the love and the things that we're positive about that make for spirituality. The need to attack and to exercise our will on people has nothing to do with spirituality. It has to do with the inability to function as a human being, to keep your tensions inside yourself, to really use that energy and rise above it, not to malign the atmosphere and not to attack anyone else. Regardless of how bad you think your problem is, you have to come with some dignity. You have to come having worked and drawn within yourself and risen a little above the situation. If this lady on the airplane with no spiritual life could gather herself together and travel alone, then there's no excuse for any of us.

Life hasn't been that bad for any of you. The simple dignity that every human being should be responsible for in life has to do with good manners and consideration. You have to exercise that in your attitude with other people. I'm tired of people squeezing me halfway to death every time they hug me. They're anxiously hugging me and choking my breath off, and this happens about fifty times a week. I never stop being amazed at this. We do this with such gusto and such love that we destroy somebody instead of opening to and honoring that person with a little detachment and a little more consideration before lunging. It really has to do with a little sensitivity.

I know that when I was younger and reached for a child, the child would be traumatized for weeks. We have to understand that even when milking a cow we will get ourselves kicked if we go about it in the wrong way. And we all have this kind of sensitivity and protectiveness. The fact is we have to love other people as they want to be loved and as they're capable of being loved. It's a simple thing that has to do with the dignity of life. Detachment is the ability to consciously draw into ourselves for a split second and rise above the situation to take a look. If I had a brace on my neck I'm sure it wouldn't make a difference to most people. They would instinctively hug me the way they want to.

You have to feel and see and understand. It's important. Creative energy can only be taken as it is and not the way you think it should be. This is what I'm working for, and I'm very grateful to understand and have no hesitancy to do it. In the same way, you have no right to interrupt whatever I'm structuring in myself. I will break down the crystallization in my life any way that it's possible. I've been working on this for years and it certainly deserves a little respect because when I free myself that way, I'll be freeing all of you in a very deep way. I'm grateful for this to happen. It's better than Weight Watchers, and it will take care of me for a long time.

* * *

I'm conscious of my purpose—and you have to be conscious of yours. Everything in me is for your growth and I'm deeply involved and conscious of your need. I wouldn't have you here any other way. I won't have anybody here who is detrimental to me and I certainly don't want to restrict another human being. I am too busy destroying my karma.

Life is simple. When you really open, you will be told by God—not by me—what your life is about. It will be there, written very clearly, because that's all we're here for. The ability to function in a simple way is to internalize your energy and release the tensions every day. This can take one minute or ten minutes depending on how strong your day has been. On an intense or violent day you may have to sit for an hour with your hands and feet down letting the negative psychic tension run off.

* * *

Don't try to push forty pounds of love onto someone with a capacity to receive only two pounds. The person will choke to death. It's like a mother compulsively feeding her child—the child is spitting out the food and gagging while the mother keeps shoving in the food. Be willing to see when somebody tries to pull back a little. Your capacity may be excessive for somebody else—or theirs may be excessive for you. Tune in, make a bridge, and feel with the other person. Don't project your illusion but see the reality. Really open from within yourself—don't just meet people and shove your love at them. Most likely they are on a different frequency than you.

* * *

What destroys most relationships are the sexual and emotional cycles that differ between people. Some people are on one-day cycles, some are on ten-week cycles, some people are on fifteen-minute cycles. The mistake comes in wanting people to perform as we need, not as they can. You can almost cut people to pieces before they will sit down and simply say, "I like this and this and this and I can't stand that and that and that." Instead we assume we know. So we chew on their funny bones and they convulse inside and become traumatized. And all you wanted was for them to open emotionally... How can they do that? You have to be very straightforward and say, "Look, I feel this. What do you feel? I want this. What do you want?" But we never do. We go through life with blinders and feel our way right over the edge of a cliff. This is dangerous and will never give us what we need.

I saw an Indian friend of mine today. For the twelve years that I studied with my last teacher, he was the person I shoveled all the information to that I wanted carried back to India. I didn't want anybody to ever say that I was anything but what I presented. And I really made it very difficult. I've always made it difficult for anybody that I dealt with because I put everything on the firing line. This may seem hard—but it's easier and definitely clearer than squirreling away and assuming somebody knows. Don't go though life assuming. Take the path of simplicity—don't hold back.

* * *

*E*veryone's physical and emotional cycles are on different timers. For instance, you come home, you want a certain kind of reception, and you start reaching for something that isn't there. And you reach for it and you even think for a few hours that you're living with it. You are so sure of what you want that you assume that the other person has it to offer. And soon you find out that you were wrong and then there's an argument—and it's all because you weren't tuned in.

I have very obvious energy cycles. But almost nobody knows or cares enough to relate to them. Instead people come in and reach for what they want. I watch this endlessly.

CHAPTER 17

*I*t is better to be potential than to be anything. And at this point, I am reduced to potential. I feel as if one great big seed is starting to grow in me, and it has nothing to do with my will. It has to do with God's will. The greatest thing we can do is to keep surrendering, to draw this energy in, to nurture inside us this thing that can grow. That is what really breaks us apart to conclude that particular level. This seed inside will then sprout and grow, allowing us to become not just an instrument for growing, but the tree of life, or that which gives forth this energy as a tree gives off oxygen. Eventually, there will be in some of you that which can grow and give off this spiritual force simply and naturally.

I was very lucky because of the Shankaracharya of Puri. One day he said to me, "On your forty-fourth birthday, this thing will start to grow in you. You won't have to talk very much. As a tree gives off oxygen, it will give off the energy that's needed. You will just walk and people will take. This will be it. You will never know or have to know."

It is not a question of will. Finally, for all of us, it is a question of being strong enough to surrender your will so that you don't know. You only know one thing—that you can surrender and allow this energy to free these higher things within you. At this point, I feel ruptured from my toes to the top of my head as this new life process takes place in me. I can make no parallel. I have never heard of one and I am not particularly interested even if there was because each one of us should have our own growth. It is not a question of me being somebody else or somebody else being me, but of just being myself. From that, this thing of God can grow. I can surrender and nourish it.

To serve this thing that is trying to grow requires inner strength. Because we do not use our energy to direct it or project it or in any way inflict it on other people, it grows organically and naturally. So if I am a little less outgoing for the next couple of weeks, it is because I have to allow this to take root as deeply as possible and grow. I don't intend to slice into the seed that is trying to grow. I will allow it to function. More than ever, I am certain about the miracle of it because it has to do with a higher will.

If you can, while you work, open very deeply and allow some of this energy to come deeply inside you. It can certainly work under similar conditions. Open deeply and feel a nothingness inside you that is complete. Open inside so that this seed can land in a place where it can grow, in a place to be a vehicle for something higher. It can't land in your mind and grow. It can't even land on your heart and grow. It has to land very deeply inside you. Try to visualize and feel and breathe and open very deeply as if you were just cut into four sections. This void inside you is what we all come from. We all branch off from this one energy. It is an energy that is very deep and, at the same time, very light—so strong that it doesn't have to be a substance. It is a thing of refinement and depth.

* * *

*I*t has always been my strength to be able to do our simple breathing exercise for a long period of time, allowing it to go deeper and deeper. It is this basic work that is the foundation of spirituality—improvising is no substitute for longevity and discipline. It is the inability of students—or teachers—to continue to do the work given them over time that brings failure.

* * *

*T*oday was particularly exhausting. I know I've been going through a transition but couldn't quite determine the nature and the way in which it would carry me. I sat for at least seven or eight hours letting negative psychic tensions flow through my fingers—and the flow seemed to be increasing. I began to feel an opening in my heart that helped pump out these tensions. As I thought about the love of the many people around me, I felt a great warmth in my heart as positive energy flowed down from my brain to my heart and into my sex chakra. This clarified the reason for the amount of outflow of negative psychic tensions. It was my system making room for the transfer of a finer energy and the removal of the heavier energy that had occupied that area previously. I feel refreshed and strong. Having to work consciously to assimilate the love that has changed my chemistry and raised my level of being seems a small price to pay.

* * *

I feel the last year of my life preparing me for the understanding that expanded consciousness can only come through expanded nothingness. It is the removal of tensions within us that allows us to expand and become an instrument through which this force can flow. This is God flowing through us and revealing our connection to him.

BIBLIOGRAPHY

A variety of books and tapes are available by and about Rudi and his teachings. They include Rudi's first book *Spiritual Cannibalism* (1973) and two volumes edited from transcripts of taped talks, *Rudi: In His Own Words* (1990) and *Rudi: Entering Infinity* (1994). Six talks (four of them edited into chapters of *Entering Infinity*) are available on audiocassette: *Rudi on Tape* is a special two-tape set on the subjects of conscious living and the wish to grow, while the *Entering Infinity* companion tape contains the raw materials for Chapters 6 and 7 of the book.

Two books about Rudi's teacher Nityananda are *Nityananda: The Divine Presence* (1984) by M. U. Hatengdi and *Nitya Sutras: The Revelations of Nityananda from the Chidakash Gita* (1985) by M. U. Hatengdi and Swami Chetanananda.

The spiritual practice of which Rudi speaks did not end with his death. Since 1973, his American student, Swami Chetanananda, has continued the tradition through the founding of the Nityananda Institute, headquartered in Portland, Oregon. His books include *Songs from the Center of the Well* (1985), *The Breath of God* (1988), *Dynamic Stillness*

(Part One): The Practice of Trika Yoga (1990), *Dynamic Stillness (Part Two): The Fulfillment of Trika Yoga* (1991), and *The Logic of Love* (1992). Available on audiotape are *Meditation: An Invitation to Inner Growth* (with practice guide) and *Keys to Mastery* (three-tape set).

For information, please contact your local library, bookstore, or Rudra Press, P.O. Box 13390, Portland, OR 97213-0390, 1-800-876-7798.

INDEX

At its core, Rudi's teaching was simple and direct. It was built on a few central concepts and themes that he approached from many different angles. Therefore, most of the headings in this index are thematic. We hope it will help readers find key concepts or favorite passages.

KEY TO CHAPTERS

Chapter 1 - January 5, 1972

Chapter 2 - January 9, 1972

Chapter 3 - January 12, 1972

Chapter 4 - January 13, 1972

Chapter 5 - January 15, 1972

Chapter 6 - January 18/19, 1972*

Chapter 7 - January 20, 1972*

Chapter 8 - January 24, 1972

Chapter 9 - January 26, 1972

Chapter 10 - February 14, 1972

Chapter 11 - January 4, 1973

Chapter 12 - January 9, 1973*

Chapter 13 - February 6, 1973

Chapter 14 - February 8, 1973

Chapter 15 - February 15, 1973*

Chapter 16 - February 20, 1973

Chapter 17 - collection

available on audio cassette